Identifying Chincoteague Ponies 2021

Cover photo taken May 2020. Front Cover: Ajax
Back Cover: Rosie's Teapot

Other books from
Jennie's Music Room Books

Nicio and Cedar Fire
Legends of Two-Legs
Identifying Chincoteague Ponies [2017]
Identifying Chincoteague Ponies 2018
Identifying Chincoteague Ponies 2019
Identifying Chincoteague Ponies 2020

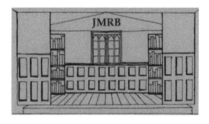

Jennie's Music Room Books
4241 Filmore St
Chincoteague Island, VA 23336

ISBN: 978-0-9842392-2-1

Contents

Preface

About This Book

The primary purpose of this book is to aid in the identification of individual members of the feral herd of horses known as Chincoteague ponies. These ponies reside on the southern Virginia end of Assateague Island. There is a completely separate herd at the northern Maryland end of the island know as Assateague horses. The Maryland herd is not included in this book.

This book is the work of one person. The author took the photos, drew the drawings, collected the data, formatted the pages and published the book.

There will be times when you will not be able to positively identify an individual using one resource. Animals with solid coats and very light pintos can be hard to identify. Colors appear differently depending on the season, weather, and lighting conditions. Long hair in the winter may obscure brands. Mud can cover legs. Manes blow around.

The author recommends that when in doubt, search the internet. She starts with the Chincoteague Pony Pedigree Database at chincoteaguepedigrees.com. Besides interesting geneology information, there are links to other web sites with photo galleries and band information. Another method is to post pictures and ask in any of the various Facebook pony groups, like I Love Chincoteague Ponies!

To report errors or to make suggestions for next year's book, please message me through my Facebook page - Chincoteague Pony Names.

Organization

Ponies are grouped alphabetically by color. **Bay**: Any dark colored horse with black points*. Colors range from shades of red to very dark brown. **Black**: An all black horse including points*. **Buckskin**: Any light colored horse with black/brown points*. Colors range from very light cream to yellow, tan, or gold. **Chestnut**: A reddish brown horse. Colors range from light red to deep mahogany. **Palomino**: A pale horse with white mane and tail. Colors range from cream to golden.

*points: legs, muzzle, mane and tail, and tips of ears

Each color is divided into 3 sections. **Solid:** A horse with no white markings on the body other than face and legs. **Comparison Chart**: Additional characteristics that might aid in identifying a solid horse. **Pinto**: A horse with white markings on the body other than face and legs. Any horse could have white on the face and legs.

Alphabetical by name, brand, and stallion indexes are included. The alphabetical index includes official names and popular nicknames.

There is also an family index which shows the relationships of the current living members of the herd. For more detailed pedigrees, refer to the Chincoteague Pony Pedigree Database at chincoteaguepedigrees.com.

Bay Girl

Fluffy
mare   birth year: 1999   brand: none
Witch Doctor x Wild Island Orchid

Brown eyes.

Notes:

Bay Girl

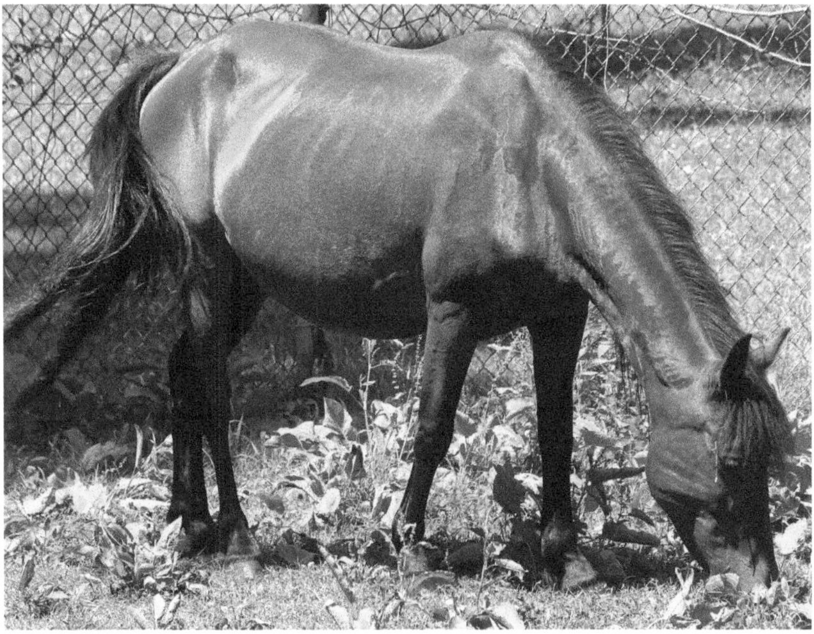

Daisey

mare   birth year: 2004   brand: none
CINNAMON HOLOGRAM x MERRY TEAPOT'S HIGH BID

Brown eyes. Sold at the 2004 auction and donated back to CVFD in 2012 by auction buyer Don Thornton. Alternate sire: Witch Doctor, Alternate dam: Wild Island Orchid.

Notes:

Daisey

Doc's Bay Dream

Bay Dream
mare birth year: 2018 brand: 18
Effie's Papa Bear x Doctor Amrien

Brown eyes. Auction price: $7,500. First seen April 5, 2018. Buyback donor: Dan and Abby Davis family, Darcy and Steve Cole, and friends of Capt Dan.

Notes:

Doc's Bay Dream

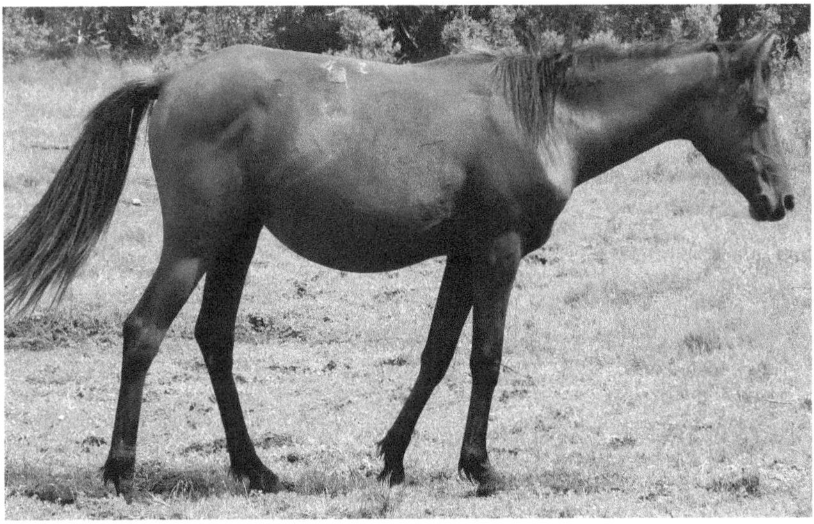

Effie's Papa Bear

Poseidon's Fury, Hoppy
stallion birth year: 2007 brand: 07
SOCKETT TO ME X MERMAID

Brown eyes. Auction price: $7,500. Born April 9, 2007. Buyback donator: Stephanie Guerlain.

Notes:

Effie's Papa Bear

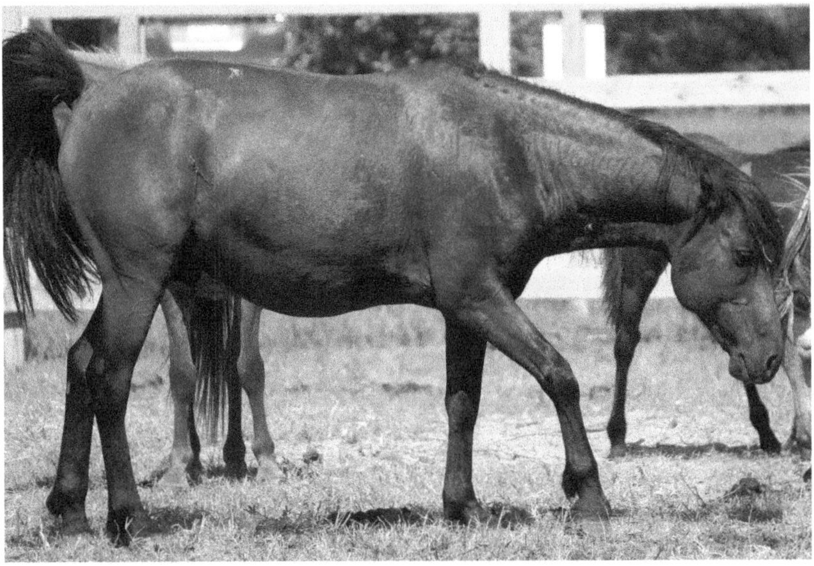

Little Dolphin

Neptune
stallion birth year: 2008 brand: 08
RAINBOW WARRIOR x LANDRIE'S GEORGIA PEACH

Brown eyes. Born May 14, 2008. King Neptune. Donated back by raffle winner.

Notes:

Little Dolphin

Pappy's Pony

mare birth year: 2003 brand: 03
OCEAN STAR x ISLAND STAR

Brown eyes. Auction price: $6,600. Born July 16, 2003. Alternate sire: Witch Doctor. Buyback donator: Stepp family.

Notes:

Pappy's Pony

Pony Ladies' Sweet Surprise

Lady
mare birth year: 2004 brand: 04
GUNNER'S MOON x SWEET INSPIRATION

Brown eyes. Auction price: $3,150. Born May 2, 2004. Buyback donator: Buyback Babes.

Notes:

Pony Ladies' Sweet Surprise

Bay

Thunderbolt

stallion birth year: 2018 brand: 18
CHIEF GOLDEN EAGLE x BLING BLING

Brown eyes. First seen May 14, 2018. Donated back to CVFC.

Notes:

Thunderbolt

Two Teagues Taco

Taco
mare birth year: 2005 brand: 05
WITCH DOCTOR x WILD ISLAND ORCHID

Brown eyes. Auction price: $5,000. Born July 12, 2005. Buyback donator: Myfe Moore.

Notes:

Two Teagues Taco

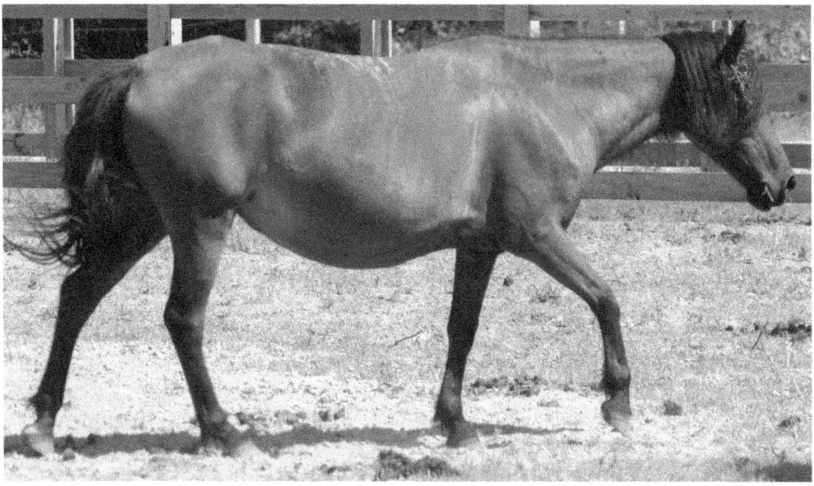

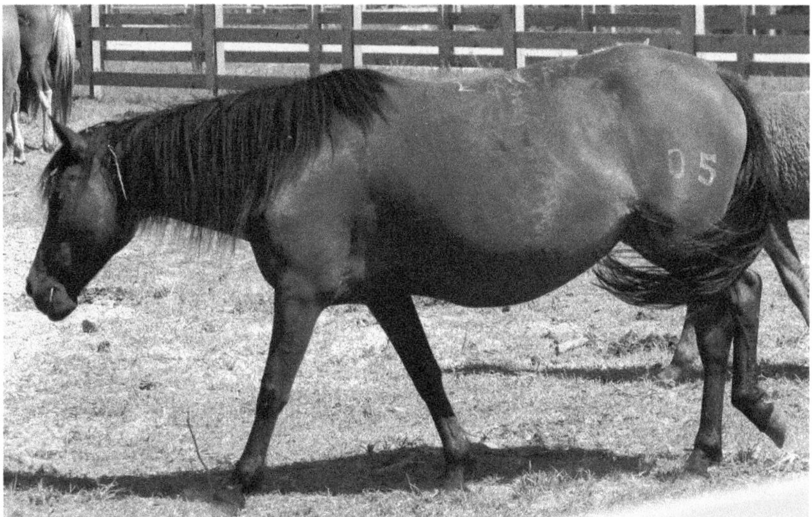

Bay

Unci

mare birth year: 1995 brand: none
(UNKNOWN) x (UNKNOWN)

Brown eyes. Swayback.

Notes:

Unci

Jean Bonde's Bayside Angel

Angel
mare birth year: 2015 brand: 15, partial
Sockett To Me x Leah's Bayside Angel

Brown eyes. Auction price: $6,400. Born April 22, 2015. Buyback donator: Buyback Babes.

Notes:

Jean Bonde's Bayside Angel

Bay

Leah's Bayside Angel

mare birth year: 1999 brand: unreadable
OCEAN STAR X SUMMER BREEZE

Brown eyes. Born July 1999. Buyback donator: In memory of Leah Potter.

Notes:

Leah's Bayside Angel

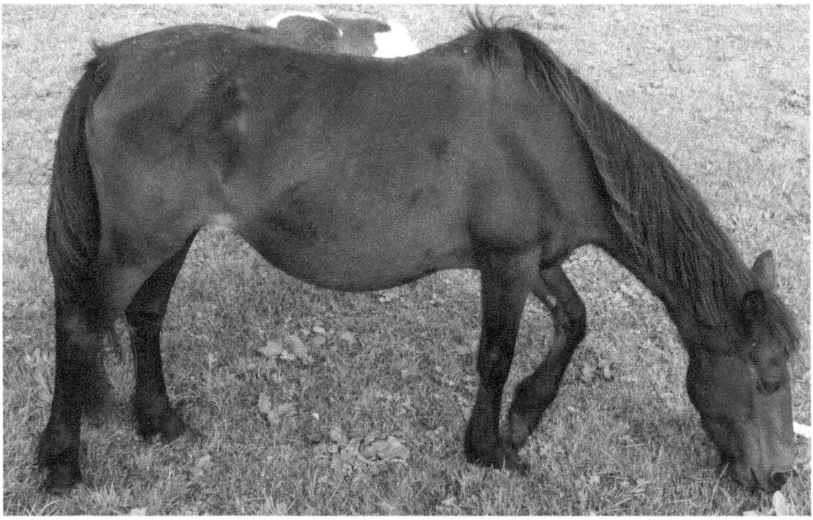

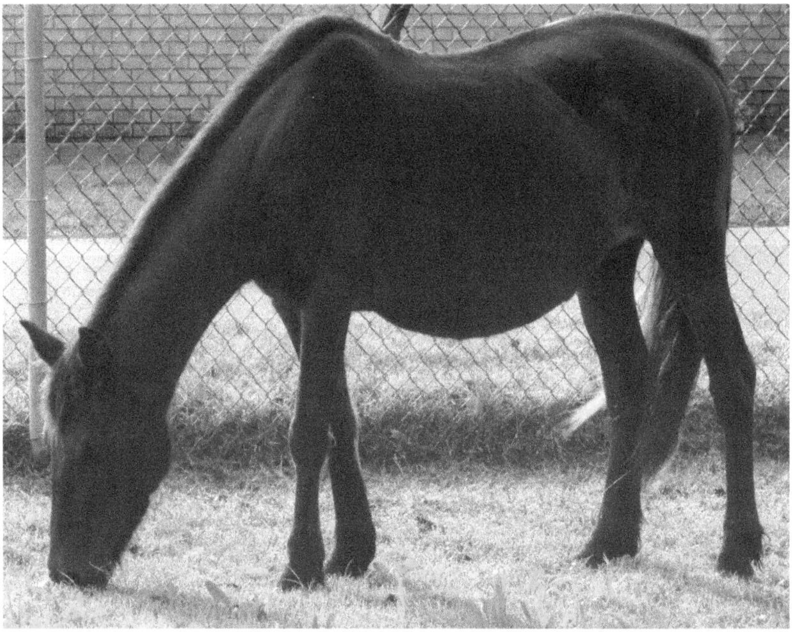

Tawny Treasure

mare   birth year: 2017   brand: 17
EFFIE'S PAPA BEAR x ISLE TREASURE

Brown eyes. Auction price: $7,100. First seen June 14, 2017. Buyback donator: Wanda and George Panos.

Notes:

Tawny Treasure

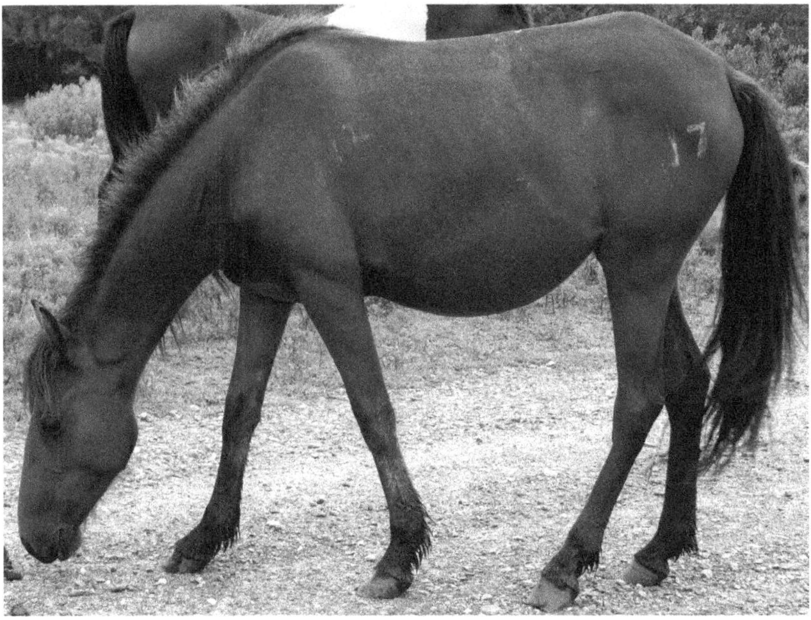

Dakota Sky's Cody Two Socks

Cody
mare birth year: 2005 brand: 05, partial
COPPER MOOSE x STEVENSON'S DAKOTA SKY

Brown eyes. Auction price: $5,000. Born May 28, 2005. Buyback donor: Catherine Young.

Notes:

Dakota Sky's Cody Two Socks

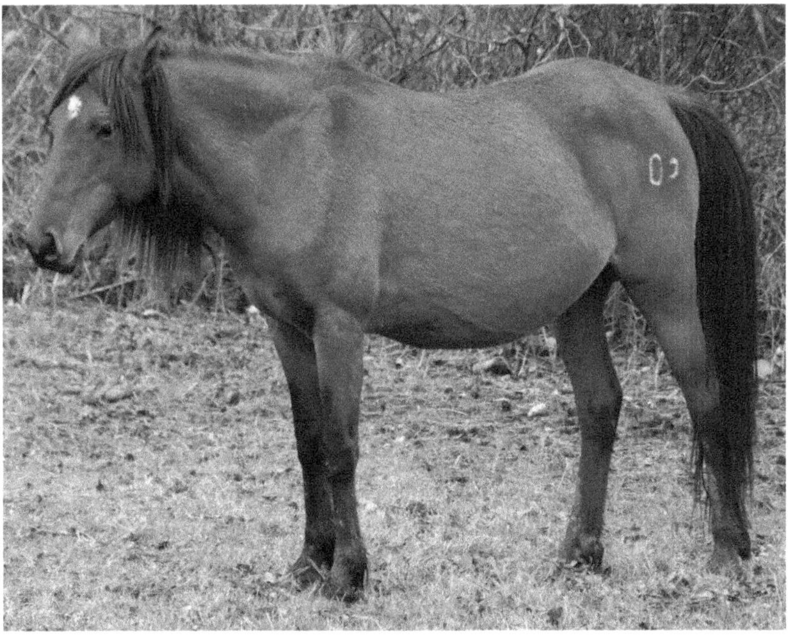

Bay Comparison Chart

Name	Pg #	Brand	Mane	Face
Bay Girl	4		left	
Daisey	6		right	
Dakota Sky's Cody Two Socks	30	05, partial	right	star
Doc's Bay Dream	8	18	left	
Effie's Papa Bear	10	07	left	
Jean Bonde's Bayside Angel	24	15, partial	left	star
Leah's Bayside Angel	26	unreadable	right	star
Little Dolphin	12	08	right	
Pappy's Pony	14	03	right	
Pony Ladies' Sweet Surprise	16	04	left	
Tawny Treasure	28	17	right	star
Thunderbolt	18	18	right	
Two Teagues Taco	20	05	left	
Unci	22		right	

NOTES

Left & right refers to the animal's left & right.

Mane: **left** = falls to the left **right** = falls to the right **split** = significant portion falls on left and right

Legs				
R F	**R B**	**L F**	**L B**	**Notable Details**
	sock		sock	upper half of 5 is gone
				stallion; very dark mane and tail
				top of 1 in brand is obscured
				stallion; small statute
				stallion; 8 looks like a 0
				swayback

R F = right front **R B** = right back **L F** = left front **L B** = left back
sock = white well below the knee **stocking** = white near and above the knee

baldface = white covers most of the face **blaze** = white streak running down the length of the face **snip** = white spot on the muzzle **star** = white spot on the forehead

Bay Pinto

Rosie's Teapot

mare birth year: 2013 brand: 13
AJAX x MOLLY'S ROSEBUD

Brown eyes. Born Fall 2013.

Notes:

Rosie's Teapot

Raindancer's Shadow of Katet

Katet
mare birth year: 2020 brand: 20
ARCHER'S GAMBIT x DESTINY FEATHERING SPIRIT

Brown eyes. First seen April 22, 2020. Buyback donor: Joanne Rome, Ginny Zelevitch, Carol Gazunis, and Olivia Wheatley.

Notes:

Raindancer's Shadow of Katet

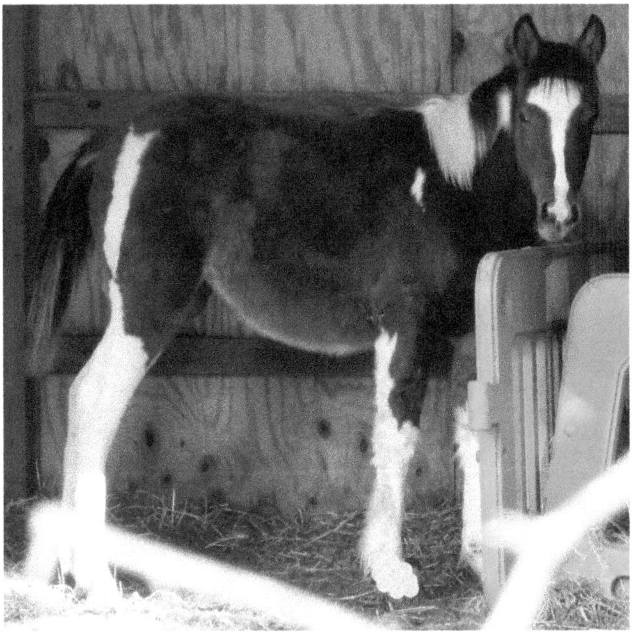

Bay Pinto

Scarlett's Little Bee

Little Bee, Bee
mare birth year: 2019 brand: 19
KEN X MAY'S GRAND SLAM

Brown eyes. Auction price: $10,000. First seen June 23, 2019. Alternate sire: Archer's Gambit. Buyback donor: Debra Evalds.

Notes:

Scarlett's Little Bee

CLG Maureen's Misty Moon

Misty Moon, Maureen
mare birth year: 2019 brand: 19
DON LEONARD STUD II x WINTER MOON

Brown eyes. Auction price: $15,000. First seen April 8, 2019. Buyback donor: Chincoteague Legacy Group. Great great great great grandfoal of Misty.

Notes:

CLG Maureen's Misty Moon

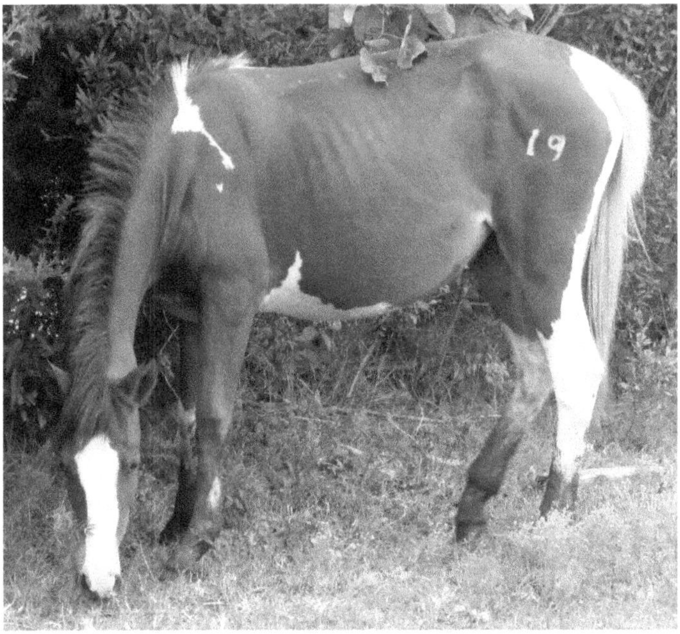

Good Golly Miss Molly

Molly
mare birth year: 2019 brand: 19
TORNADO'S LEGACY x A SPLASH OF FRECKLES

Brown eyes. Auction price: $7,400. First seen May 27, 2019.

Notes:

Good Golly Miss Molly

Summer Breeze

Cee Cee, Breezy
mare birth year: 2006 brand: none
MIRACLE MAN x BINKY'S BREEZE

Brown eyes. Born August 2006. Not auctioned, no buyback donator.

Notes:

Summer Breeze

Amari's Journey

Journey
mare birth year: 2020 brand: 20
Don Leonard Stud II x Randy

Brown eyes. Auction price: $11,600. First seen May 14, 2020. Buyback donor: Dawn and Michael Feindt.

Notes:

Amari's Journey

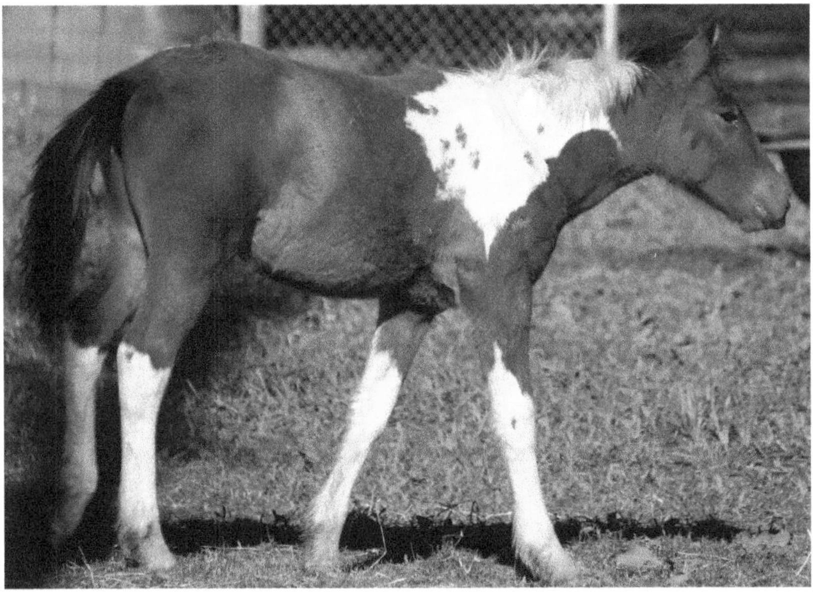

Ella of Assateague

Ella
mare birth year: 2000 brand: 00
CINNAMON HOLOGRAM x FOXY ASSET

Brown eyes. Born July 2000. Buyback donator: Cara Rosenbaum.

Notes:

Ella of Assateague

Bay Pinto

Billy Maez Renegade

Maezie
mare birth year: 2020 brand: 20
ARCHER'S GAMBIT x SCOTTY ET

Brown eyes. Auction price: $13,100. First seen April 3, 2020. Buyback donor: Steph and Kevin Neyer.

Notes:

Billy Maez Renegade

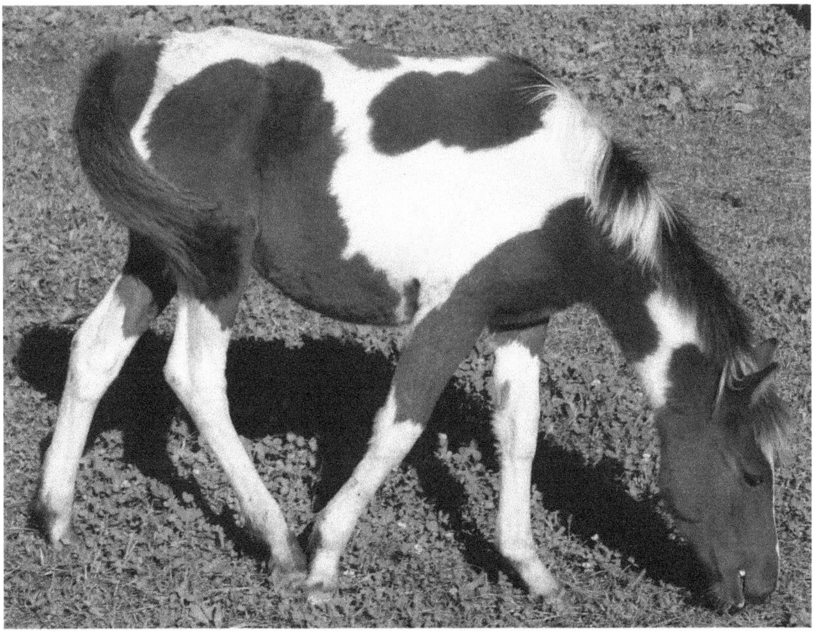

Doctor Amrien

Doc
mare birth year: 2014 brand: 14
WILD THING x DAKOTA SKY'S CODY TWO SOCKS

Brown eyes. Born September 1, 2014. Buyback donor: Dan and Abby Davis family.

Notes:

Doctor Amrien

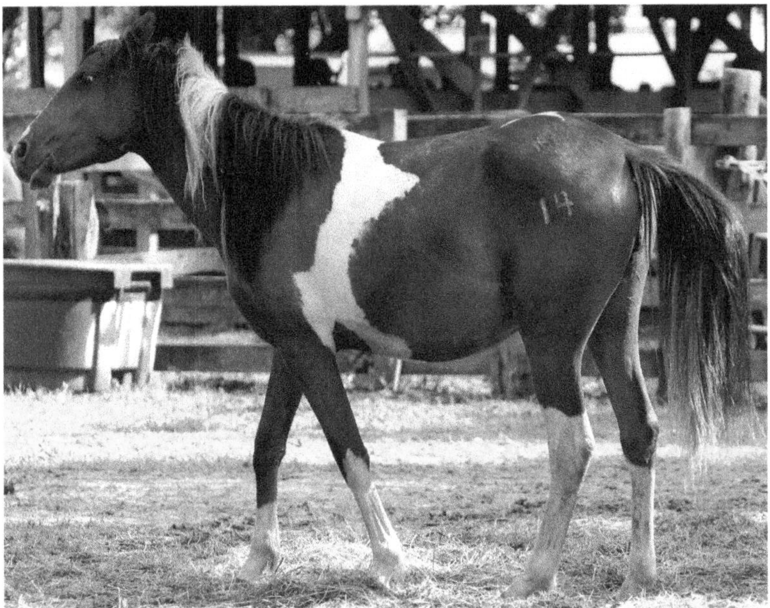

Bay Pinto

White Saddle

mare birth year: 2013 brand: 13
WITCH DOCTOR X WILD ISLAND ORCHID

Brown eyes. Auction price: $4,100. Born April 5, 2013. Buyback donator: Joan Bradley.

Notes:

White Saddle

Miracle's Natural Beauty

Natural Beauty
mare birth year: 2009 brand: 09
MIRACLE MAN x NATURAL INNOCENCE

Brown eyes. Auction price: $3,100. Born April 30, 2009. Buyback donator: Debbie and Landrie Folsom.

Notes:

Miracle's Natural Beauty

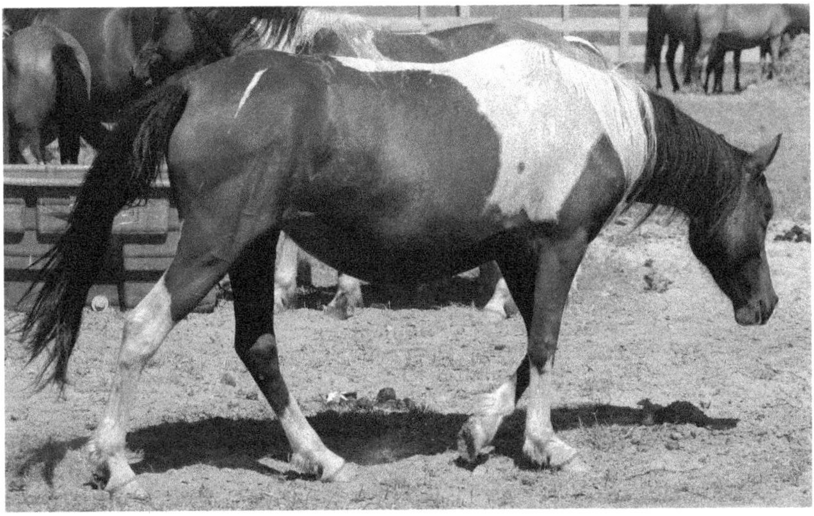

Bay Pinto

May's Grand Slam

May
mare birth year: 2012 brand: 12
MIRACLE MAN x SPANISH ANGEL

Brown eyes. Auction price: $4,700. Born April 23, 2012. Buyback donator: Loveland family.

Notes:

May's Grand Slam

Bay Pinto

Tunie

Queenie
mare birth year: 2003 brand: 03
WILLIE'S MAJESTIC DREAMER x SEASIDE

Brown eyes. Born July 7, 2003. Queen Neptune. Donated back by raffle winner.

Notes:

Tunie

Wendy's Carolina Girl

Carolina Girl
mare birth year: 2018 brand: 18
MAVERICK x ESSIE

Brown eyes. Auction price: $6,500. First seen May 14, 2018. Buyback donator: Wendy Sloan.

Notes:

Wendy's Carolina Girl

Ajax

stallion birth year: 2007 brand: 07, partial
YANKEE SPIRIT x FOXY ASSET

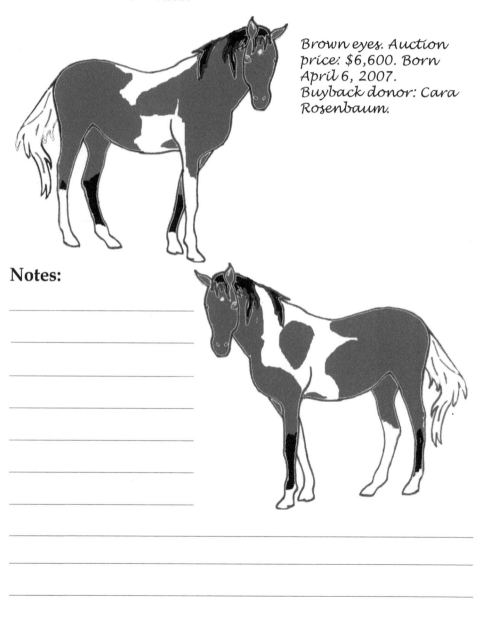

Brown eyes. Auction price: $6,600. Born April 6, 2007. Buyback donor: Cara Rosenbaum.

Notes:

Ajax

Bay Pinto

MissMe

mare birth year: 2017 brand: 17
AJAX x MIRACLE'S NATURAL BEAUTY

Brown eyes. Auction price: $13,500. First seen May 19, 2017.

Notes:

MissMe

Bay Pinto

Norman Rockwell Giddings

Norm, Rocky
stallion birth year: 2018 brand: none
ARCHER'S GAMBIT X BABE

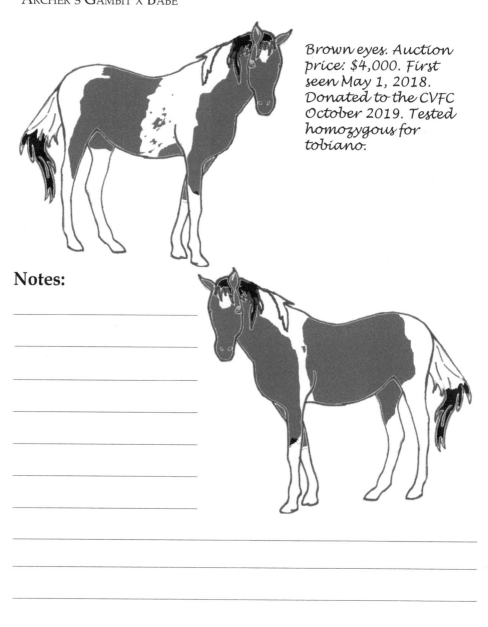

Brown eyes. Auction price: $4,000. First seen May 1, 2018. Donated to the CVFC October 2019. Tested homozygous for tobiano.

Notes:

Norman Rockwell Giddings

Bay Pinto

Sissy

mare birth year: 2019 brand: 19
Effie's Papa Bear x Splash

Brown eyes. Auction price: $16,000. First seen April 1, 2019.

Notes:

Sissy

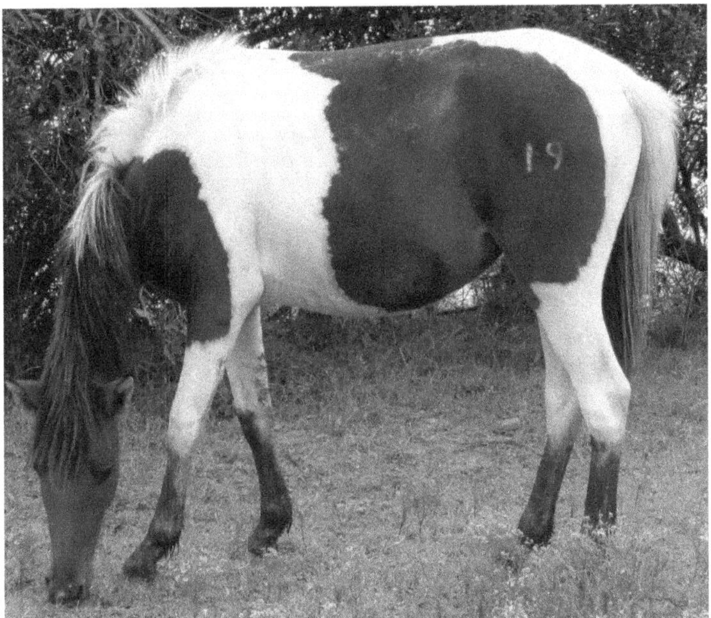

Rainbow Warrior

Napolean
stallion   birth year: 1997   brand: none
(UNKNOWN) X (UNKNOWN)

Brown eyes.

Notes:

Rainbow Warrior

Bay Pinto

Destiny Feathering Spirit

Destiny
mare   birth year: 2002   brand: none
Courtney's Boy x Vixen

Brown eyes. Born August 2002. Buyback donor: Joann Rome and Ginny Zlevitch.

Notes:

Destiny Feathering Spirit

Bay Pinto

Sweetheart

mare birth year: 2011 brand: unreadable
WILD BILL x SCOTTY ET

Brown eyes. Auction price: $4,650. Born April 18, 2011. Buyback donator: Patty.

Notes:

Sweetheart

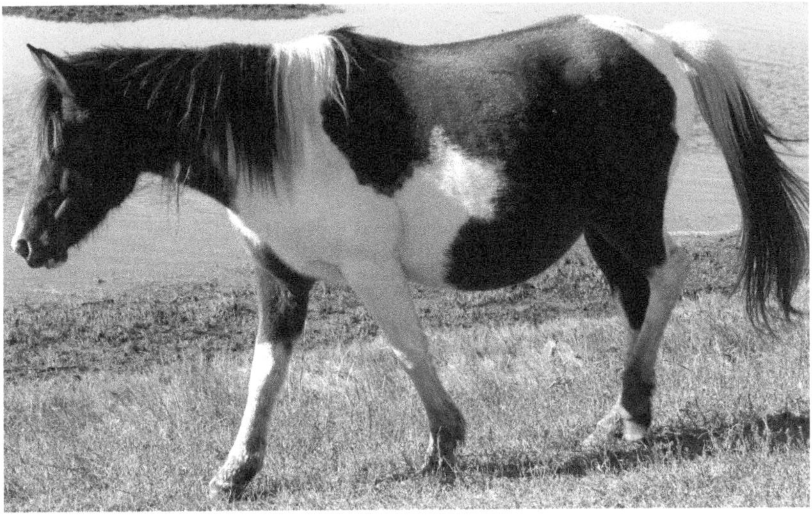

Bay Pinto

Henry's Hidalgo

stallion birth year: 2017 brand: 17
Wild Thing x Thetis

Brown eyes. Auction price: $8,900. First seen May 14, 2017. Buyback donator: Arthur Leonard.

Notes:

Henry's Hidalgo

Splash

Danny's Girl
mare birth year: 2014 brand: 14
WILD THING x SUMMER BREEZE

Brown eyes. Auction price: $7,100. Buyback donator: Beer Family.

Notes:

Splash

Bay Pinto

Grandma's Dream

mare birth year: 2013 brand: 13

WILD THING x GALADRIEL

Brown eyes. Auction price: $4,600. Born May 7, 2013. Buyback donator: Frances Bidoglio.

Notes:

Grandma's Dream

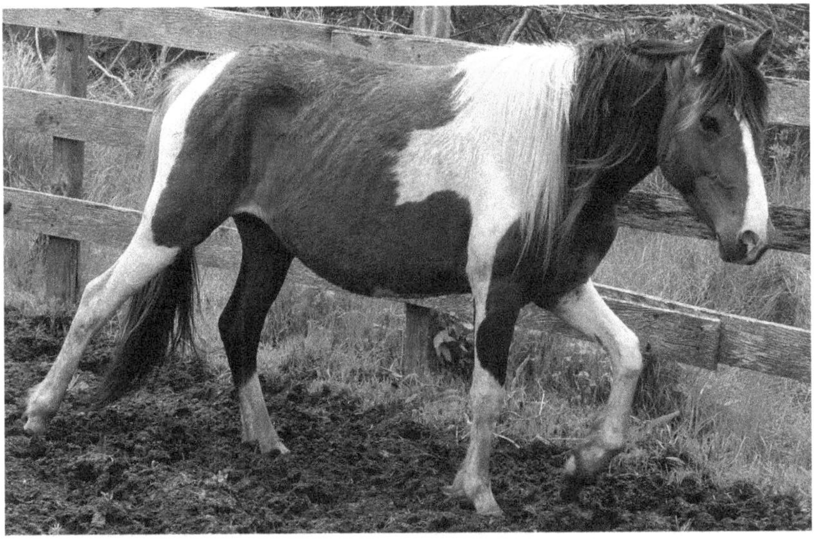

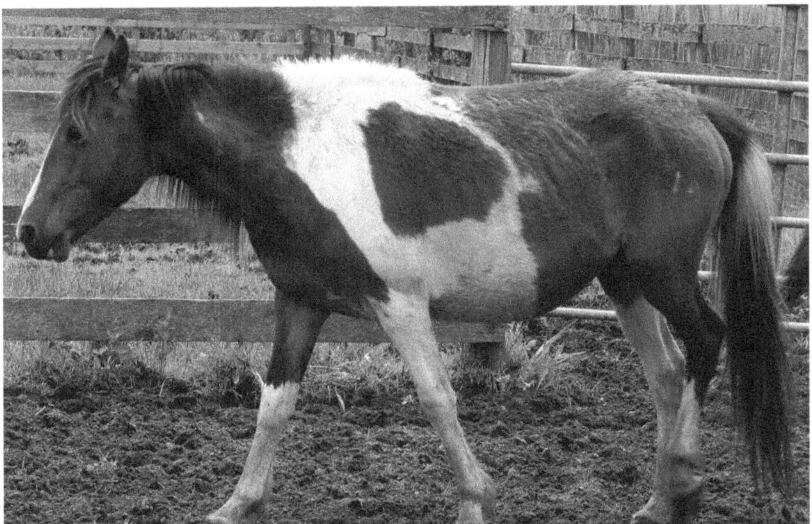

Loveland's Secret Feather

Secret, Feather
mare birth year: 2012 brand: 12
WILD THING x GALADRIEL

Brown eyes. Auction price: $7,200. Born May 1, 2012. Buyback donator: Loveland family.

Notes:

Loveland's Secret Feather

Bay Pinto

Wild Thing

stallion   birth year: 1997   brand: none
HURRICANE x JUST MY STYLE

Brown eyes.

Notes:

Wild Thing

Bay Pinto

Chickadee

mare birth year: 2013 brand: 13
Courtney's Boy x Black Star

Brown eyes. Auction price: $5,000. Born April 15, 2013. Buyback donor: Janey Beer.

Notes:

Chickadee

Bay Pinto

Wildest Dreams

mare   birth year: 2008   brand: 08

MIRACLE MAN x NATURAL INNOCENCE

Brown eyes. Auction price: $7,200. Born April 28, 2008.

Notes:

Wildest Dreams

Bay Pinto

Black Star

mare birth year: 1998 brand: none
WITCH DOCTOR x RAP THE WIND

Brown eyes. Born August 1998.

Notes:

Black Star

Bay Pinto

Marguerite of Chincoteague

mare birth year: 2013 brand: 13

TORNADO'S LEGACY x MIRACLE'S NATURAL BEAUTY

Brown eyes. Auction price: $5,800. Born April 25, 2013. Alternate sire: Archer's Gambit. Buyback donator: Ellen Wycoski.

Notes:

Marguerite of Chincoteague

Shy Anne

Half n Half
mare birth year: 1999 brand: none
HOT AIR BALLOON x SUNSHINE

Brown eyes. Born July 1999. Buyback donator: McCaskill family.

Notes:

Shy Anne

Fifteen Friends of Freckles

Freckles
mare birth year: 2006 brand: 06
NORTH STAR x MARK'S ISLAND LIBERTY

One blue, one brown eye. Auction price: $7,500. Born May 15, 2006. Buyback donator: Buyback Babes.

Notes:

Fifteen Friends of Freckles

Bay Pinto

Skylark

mare birth year: 2011 brand: none
WILD THING x FOXY ASSET

Brown eyes. Auction price: $4,000. Born May 24, 2011. Buyback donator: Kathleen Cahall.

Notes:

Skylark

Scotty ET

ET
mare birth year: 2002 brand: 02, partial
Attitude x Black Star

Brown eyes. Auction price: $4,300. Born May 5, 2002. Buyback donator: Jean Bonde.

Notes:

Scotty ET

Winter Moon

Moon
mare birth year: 2012 brand: none
CYCLONE II x HEART OF THE BAY

One blue, one brown eye. Born January 12, 2012. Donated to CVFC March 2018. Great great great grandfoal of Misty.

Notes:

Winter Moon

Bay Pinto

Sky Dancer

mare   birth year: 2019   brand: 19

AJAX X SKYLARK

Blue eyes. Auction price: $6,400. First seen July 13, 2019. Buyback donor: Liane Pfeiffer.

Notes:

Sky Dancer

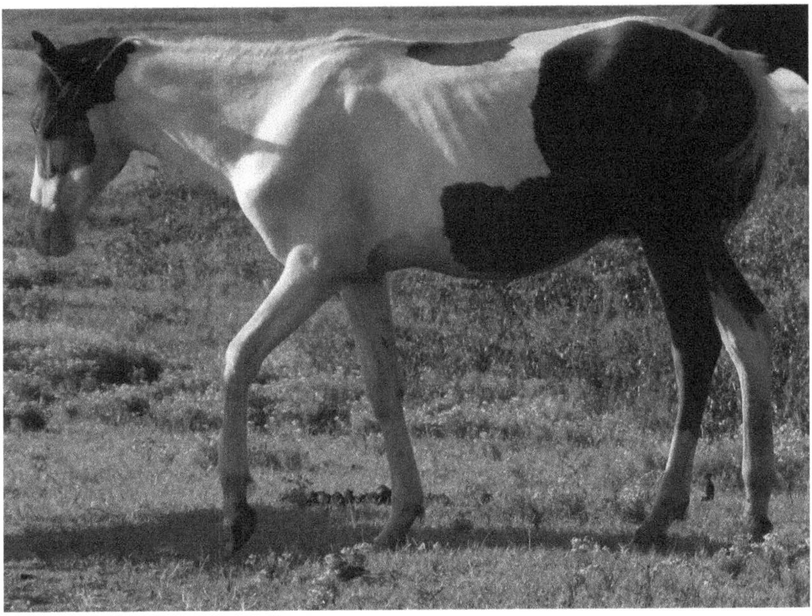

Bay Pinto

Summer

mare birth year: 2015 brand: none
WH Nightwind x Justa Kickamazoo

Brown eyes. Donated to the CVFC March 2018. Great Great Great Grandfoal of Misty.

Notes:

Summer

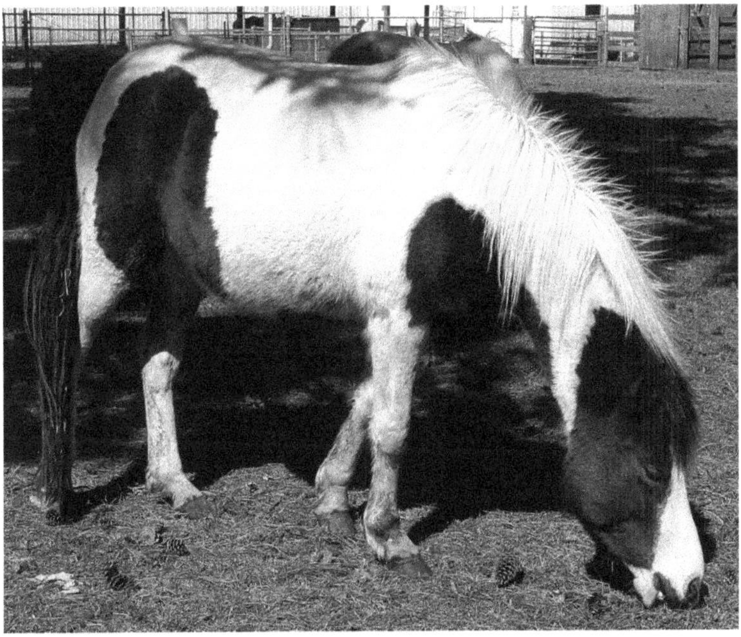

Bay Pinto

Seaside Miracle

mare birth year: 2011 brand: F
MIRACLE MAN x SEASIDE

Brown eyes. Auction price: $4,600. Born May 7, 2011.

Notes:

Seaside Miracle

A Splash of Freckles

Splash of Freckles
mare birth year: 2011 brand: unreadable
DON LEONARD STUD X FIFTEEN FRIENDS OF FRECKLES

Brown eyes. Auction price: $6,700. Born June 25, 2011. Buyback donor: Buyback Babes.

Notes:

A Splash of Freckles

Bay Pinto

Maverick

stallion birth year: 2013 brand: 14
WILD THING x WITCH KRAFT

Brown eyes. Auction price: $12,700. Buyback donator: Catherine Miller. Born December 2013, sold at 2014 auction.

Notes:

Maverick

Got Milk

Anna
mare birth year: 2000 brand: none
WITCH DOCTOR x WATERKOLOR

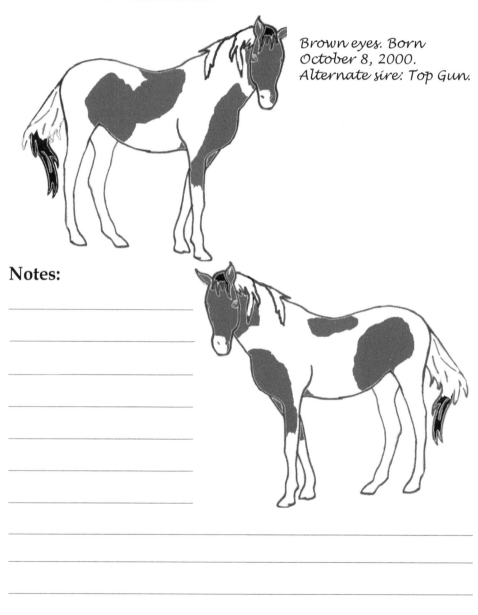

Brown eyes. Born October 8, 2000. Alternate sire: Top Gun.

Notes:

Got Milk

BAY PINTO

Heide's Sky

mare birth year: 2017 brand: none

KEN x FIFTEEN FRIENDS OF FRECKLES

Blue eyes. First seen August 21, 2017. Buyback donator: Cindy Wolfe.

Notes:

Heide's Sky

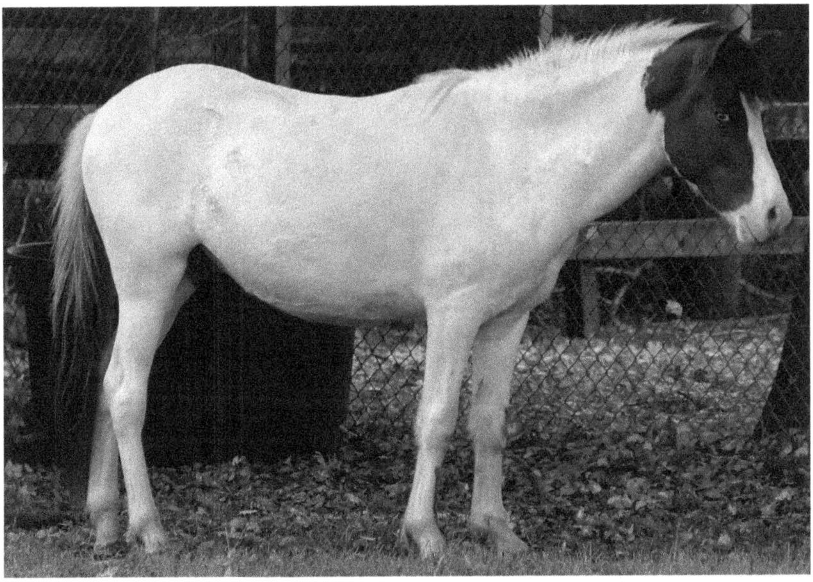

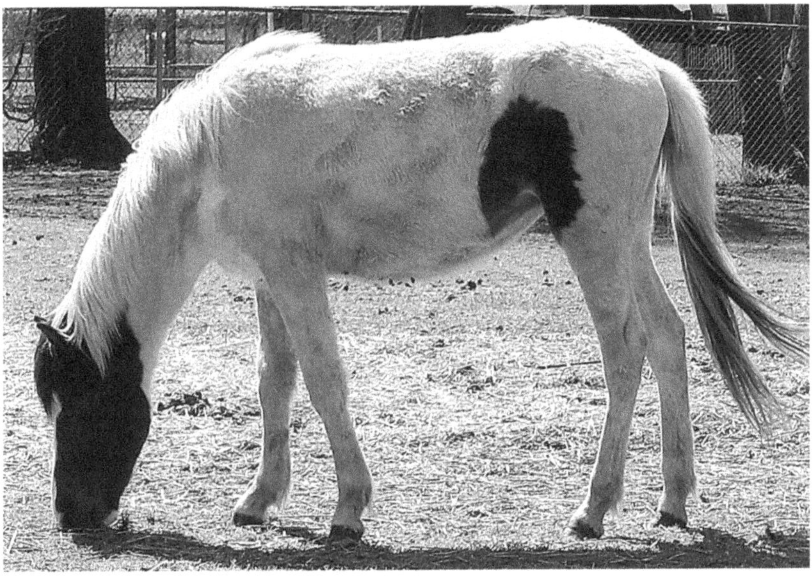

CLG Ember

Ember
mare birth year: 2018 brand: 18
SURFER'S RIPTIDE x BLACK PEARL

Brown eyes. Auction price: $11,000. First seen April 29, 2018. Buyback donor: Chincoteague Legacy Group.

Notes:

CLG Ember

Dexter's Midnight Runner

Dexie
mare birth year: 2019 brand: 19
MAVERICK X BLACK PEARL

Brown eyes. Auction price: $17,500. First seen June 5, 2019.

Notes:

Dexter's Midnight Runner

Talia/Evan's Angel

Evan's Angel, Talia
mare birth year: 2017 brand: 17
MAVERICK X SURFIN' CHANTEL

Brown eyes. Auction price: $7,400. First seen May 21, 2017. Buyback donator: Greg and Lissa St. Claire.

Notes:

Talia/Evan's Angel

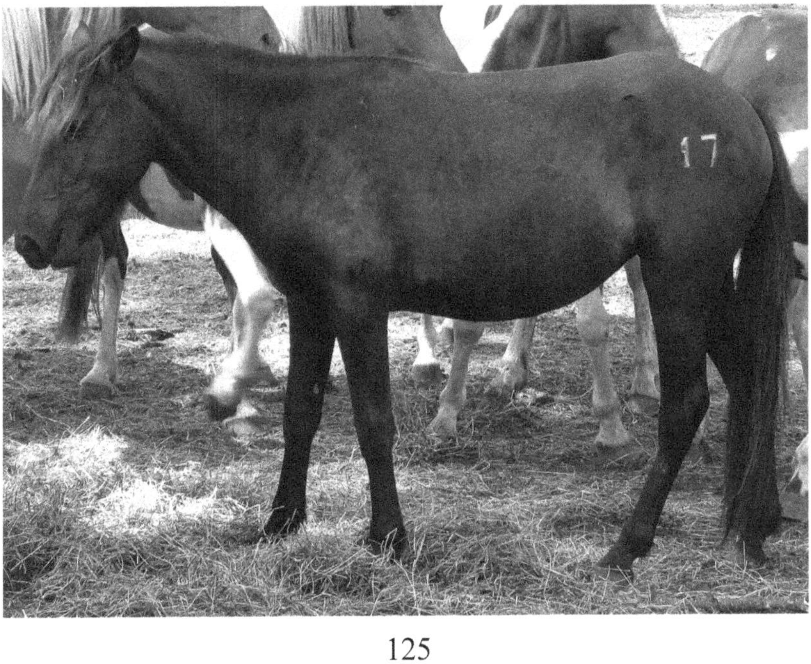

Black

Milly Sue

mare birth year: 2017 brand: 17

Surfer's Riptide x Leah's Bayside Angel

Brown eyes. Auction price: $9,000. First seen April 29, 2017.

Notes:

Milly Sue

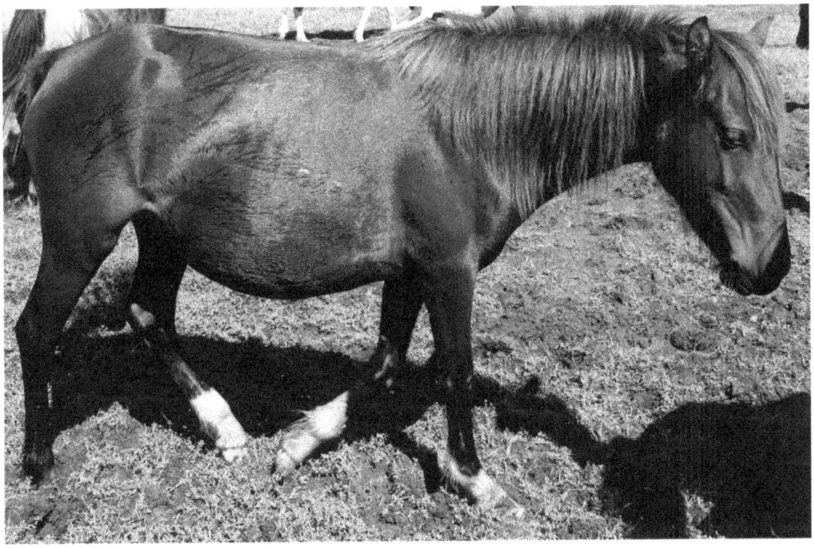

CLG Surfer's Blue Moon

Blue, Blue Moon, Surfer's Blue Moon
mare birth year: 2015 brand: 15
SURFER DUDE X GOT MILK

Blue eyes. Auction price: $25,000. Born April 27, 2015. Buyback donor: Chincoteague Legacy Group.

Notes:

CLG Surfer's Blue Moon

Black Comparison Chart

Name	Pg #	Brand	Mane	Face	
Ace's Black Tie Affair	134	07	right		
CLG Ember	120	18	left		
CLG Surfer's Blue Moon	128	15	even	baldface	
Dexter's Midnight Runner	122	19	right		
Milly Sue	126	17	right		
Talia/Evan's Angel	124	17	right		

NOTES

Ace's Black Tie Affair is included here even though he is technically a pinto. His markings are so minimal that he is routinely wrongly identified as solid black.

Left & right refers to the animal's left & right.

Mane: **left** = falls to the left **right** = falls to the right **split** = significant portion falls on left and right

Legs				Notable Details
R F	**R B**	**L F**	**L B**	
sock	stocking	sock	stocking	stallion; small upside heart behind left front leg
sock	sock	sock	sock	blue eyes
sock		sock	sock	7 in brand easily mistaken for 1

R F = right front **R B** = right back **L F** = left front **L B** = left back
sock = white well below the knee **stocking** = white near and above the knee

baldface = white covers most of the face **blaze** = white streak running down the length of the face **snip** = white spot on the muzzle **star** = white spot on the forehead

Ace's Miss Raven Rhapsody

Raven Rhapsody, Raven
mare birth year: 2020 brand: 20
ACE'S BLACK TIE AFFAIR x MARINA'S MARSH MALLOW

Brown eyes. Auction price: $28,250. First seen June 19, 2020. Buyback donor: Audra, Alexandra, and Teresa Swain.

Notes:

Ace's Miss Raven Rhapsody

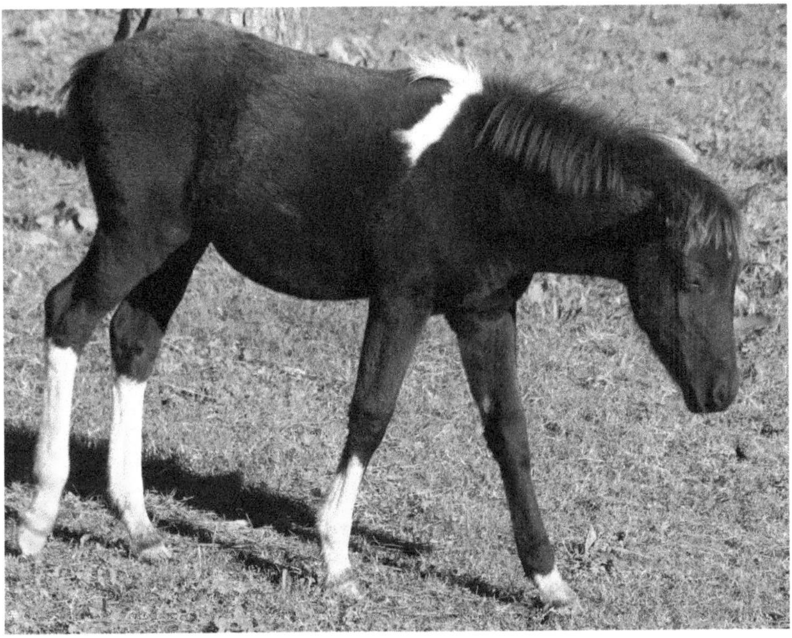

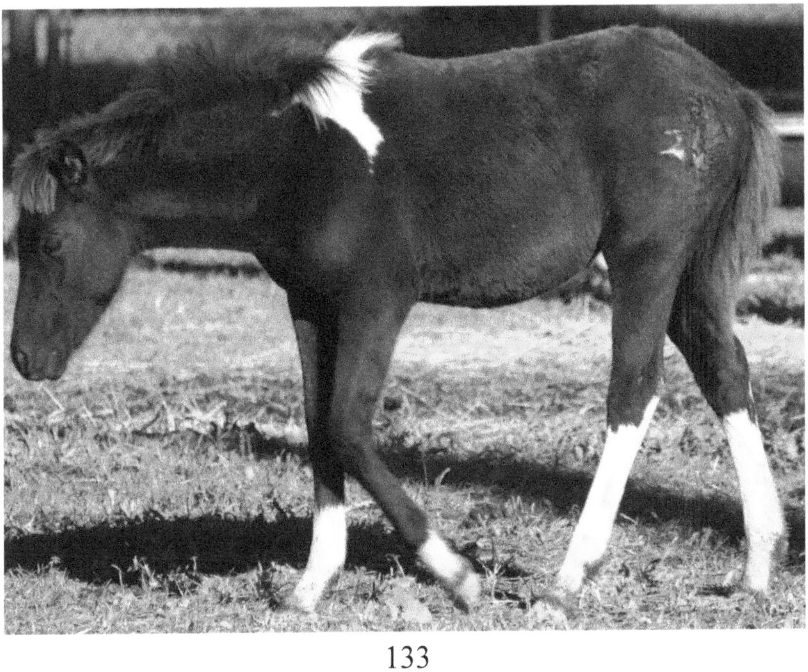

Ace's Black Tie Affair

Ace
stallion birth year: 2007 brand: 07
CENTAUR x SUSIE Q

Brown eyes. Auction price: $9,500. Born May 1, 2007. Buyback donor: Folsom family. Alternate sire: Charcoal/N9BNZ.

Notes:

Ace's Black Tie Affair

Poco's Starry Night

Starry Night, Cash
mare birth year: 2012 brand: 12
DON LEONARD STUD x POCO LATTE PW

Brown eyes. Auction price: $6,700. Born April 9, 2012. Buyback donator: Buyback Babes.

Notes:

Poco's Starry Night

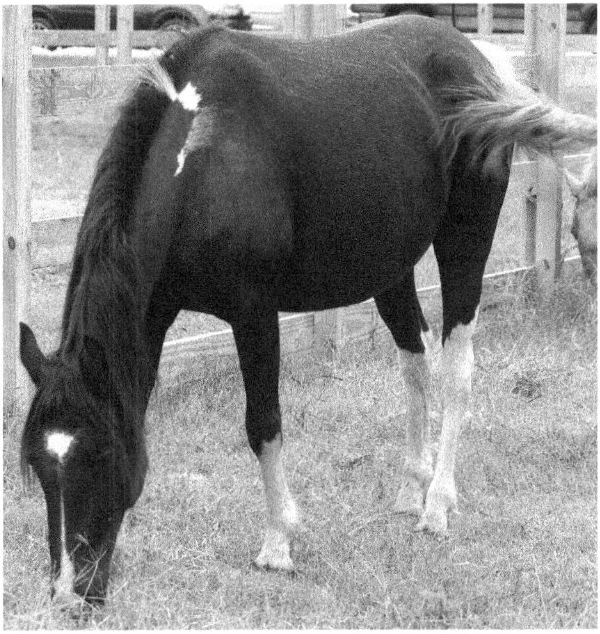

Black Pinto

Pixie Dust

mare birth year: 2014 brand: 14
ACE'S BLACK TIE AFFAIR x ANGEL WINGS

Brown eyes. Born August 29, 2014. Buyback donator: Brett Emmerson.

Notes:

Pixie Dust

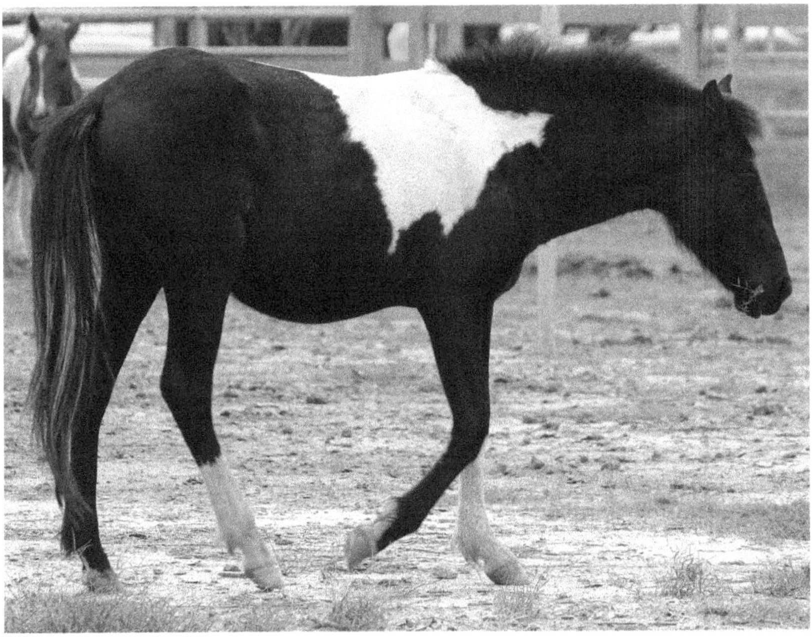

Black Pinto

Gracey

mare birth year: 2013 brand: 13
Sockett To Me x Leah's Bayside Angel

Brown eyes. Auction price: $12,000. Born April 16, 2013. Buyback donator: Mark Zebley/ Janet Marabito.

Notes:

Gracey

Black Pearl

Pearl
mare birth year: 2014 brand: 14
SOCKETT TO ME x LEAH'S BAYSIDE ANGEL

Brown eyes. Auction price: $21,000. Buyback donor: Catherine Miller.

Notes:

Black Pearl

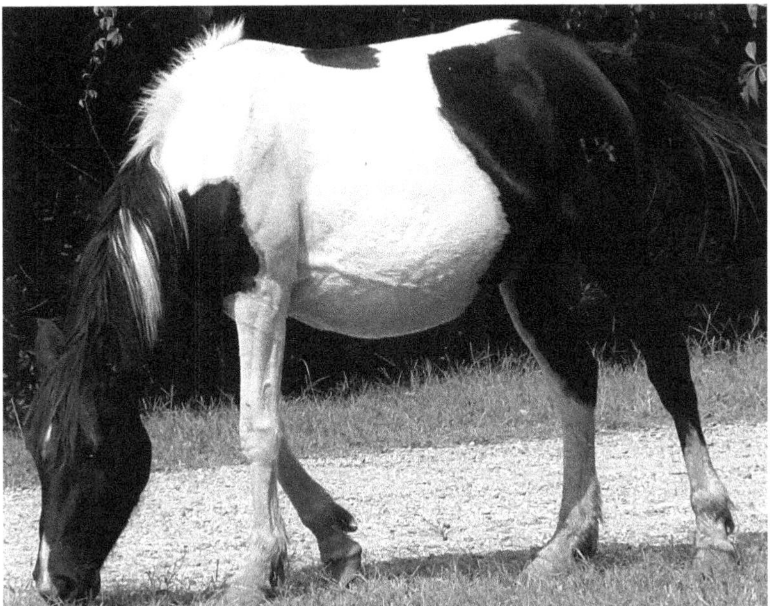

Baybe

Baby
mare birth year: 2006 brand: none
TUFFER THAN LEATHER x APRIL MOON

Brown eyes. Donated to the CVFD in 2011 by the Leonard Family.

Notes:

Baybe

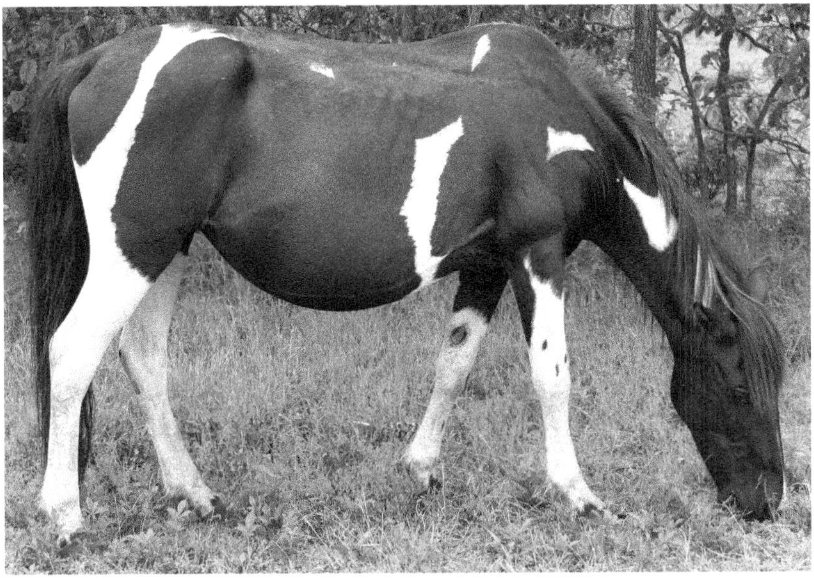

Black Pinto

Calendar Girl

mare birth year: 2017 brand: 17
WH NIGHTWIND x (UNKNOWN)

Born May 22, 2017. Donated to CVFC March 2018. Great Great Great Grandfoal of Misty.

Notes:

Calendar Girl

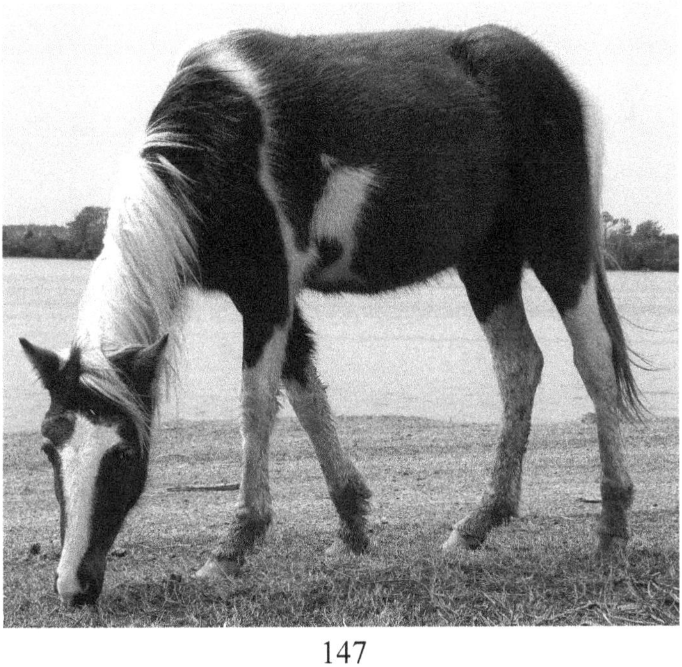

CLG Magic Moment

Magic, Magic Moment
mare birth year: 2020 brand: 20
TORNADO'S LEGACY x A SPLASH OF FRECKLES

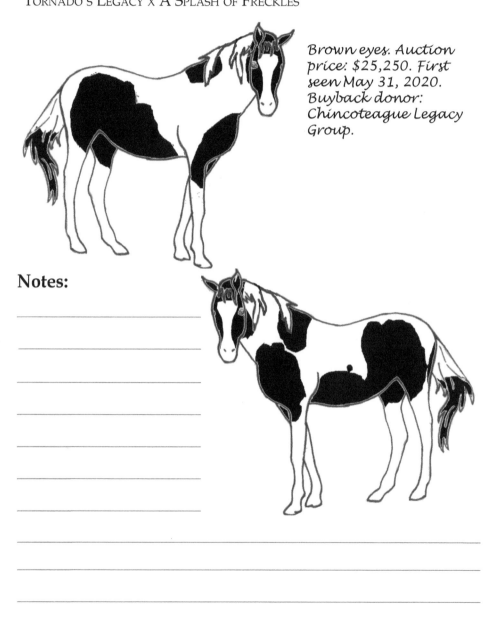

Brown eyes. Auction price: $25,250. First seen May 31, 2020. Buyback donor: Chincoteague Legacy Group.

Notes:

CLG Magic Moment

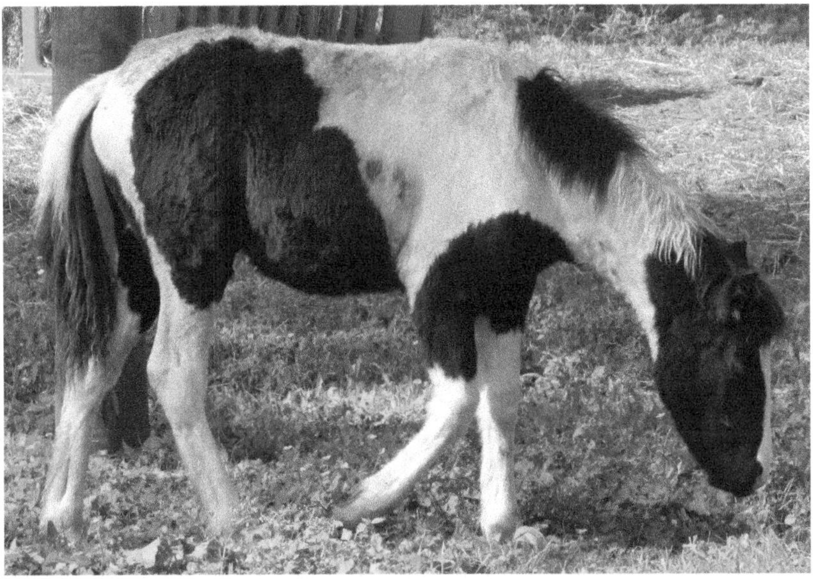

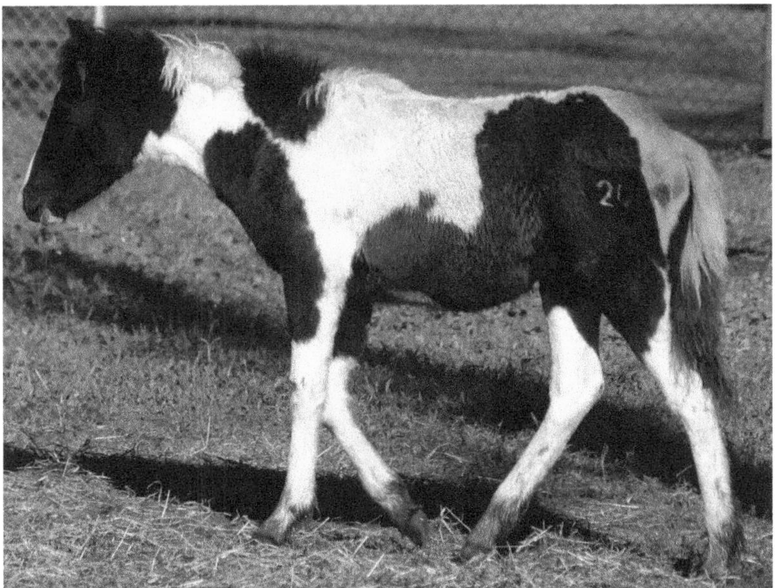

Beach Boy

Saltwater Renegade, Renegade
stallion birth year: 2015 brand: 15
WH Nightwind x WH Sea Breeze

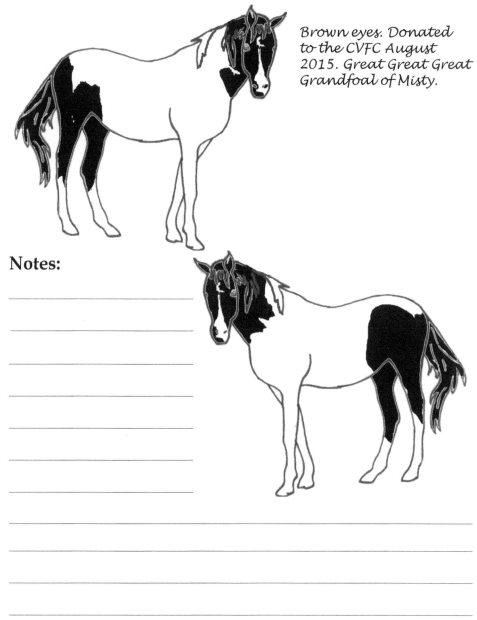

Brown eyes. Donated to the CVFC August 2015. Great Great Great Grandfoal of Misty.

Notes:

Beach Boy

Buckskin

Alice's Sandcastle

mare birth year: 2012 brand: 12
NORTH STAR x LIVING LEGEND

Brown eyes. Auction price: $5,300. Born April 27, 2012. Buyback donor: Carol Dennis.

Notes:

Alice's Sandcastle

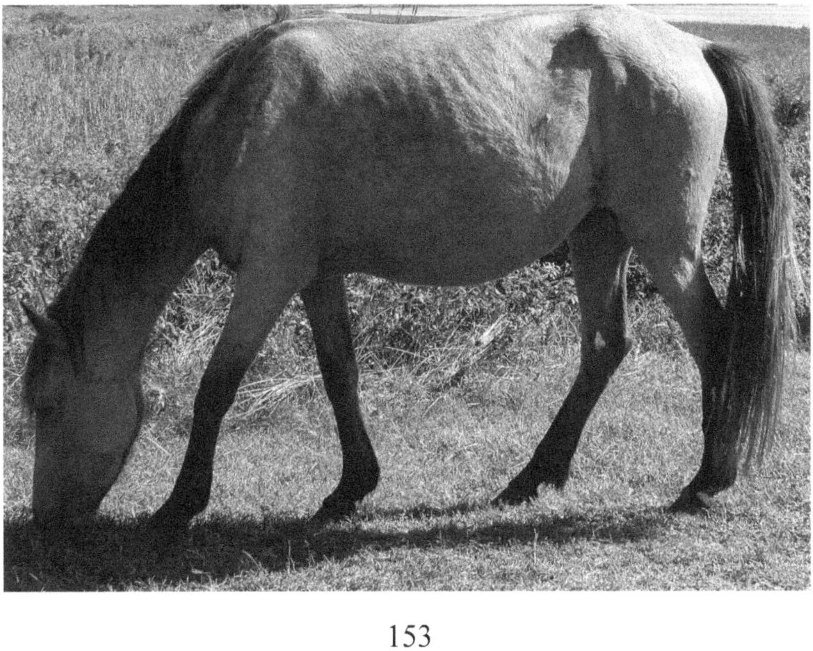

Anne Bonny's Little Flower

Flower
mare birth year: 2019 brand: 19
TORNADO'S LEGACY x ANNE BONNY

Brown eyes. Auction price: $12,500. First seen June 19, 2019. Buyback donor: Buy Back Babes.

Notes:

Anne Bonny's Little Flower

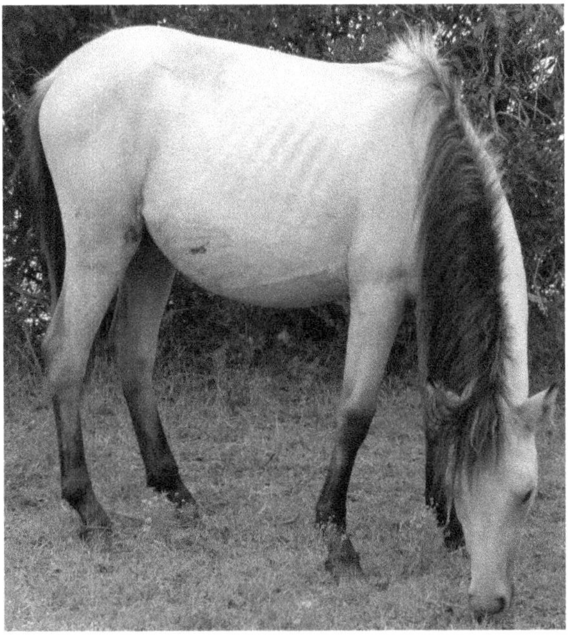

CLG Rider on the Storm

Rider, Storm
stallion birth year: 2019 brand: 19
TORNADO'S LEGACY x MIRACLE'S NATURAL BEAUTY

Brown eyes. Auction price: $16,500. First seen April 15, 2019. Buyback donor: Chincoteague Legacy Group.

Notes:

CLG Rider on the Storm

Ivana Marie Zustan

Zustan
mare   birth year: 2016   brand: 16
Little Dolphin x Jessica's Sea Star Sandy

Brown eye. Auction price: $5,700. Born May 19, 2016.

Notes:

Ivana Marie Zustan

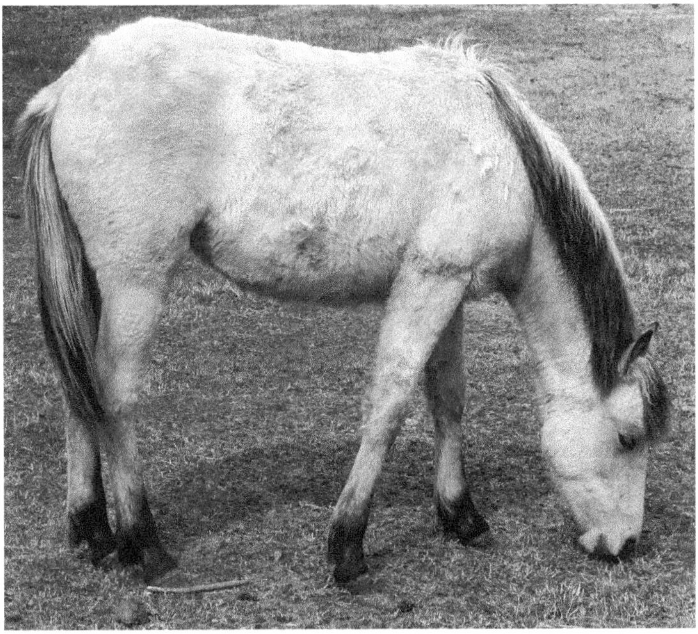

Jessica's Sea Star Sandy

Jessica's Sandy
mare birth year: 2006 brand: 06
TORNADO X PHILLY GIRL

Brown eyes. Auction price: $5,300. Born May 17, 2006. Buyback donator: Debbie Elliott-Fisk.

Notes:

Jessica's Sea Star Sandy

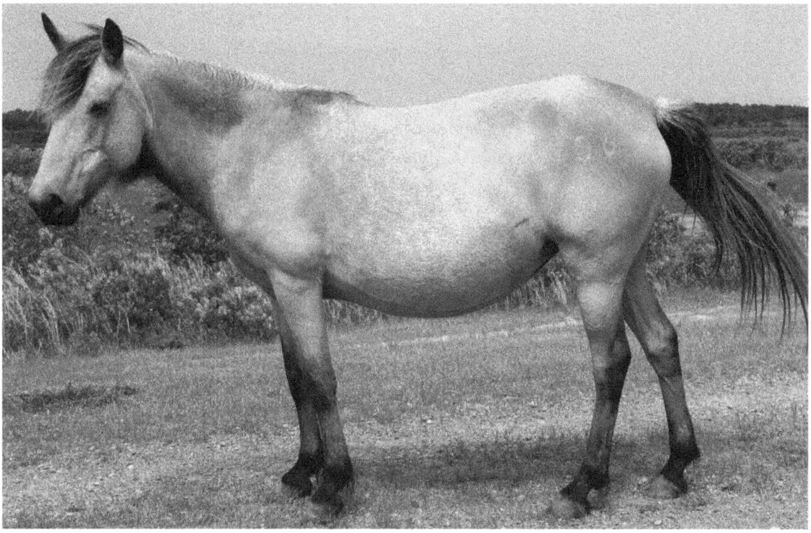

Buckskin

Liz's Serenity

Serenity
mare birth year: 2017 brand: 17
Wild Bill x Landrie's Georgia Peach

Brown eyes. Auction price: $10,000. First seen April 26, 2017. Buyback donor: In memory of Liz Spino by family and friends.

Notes:

Liz's Serenity

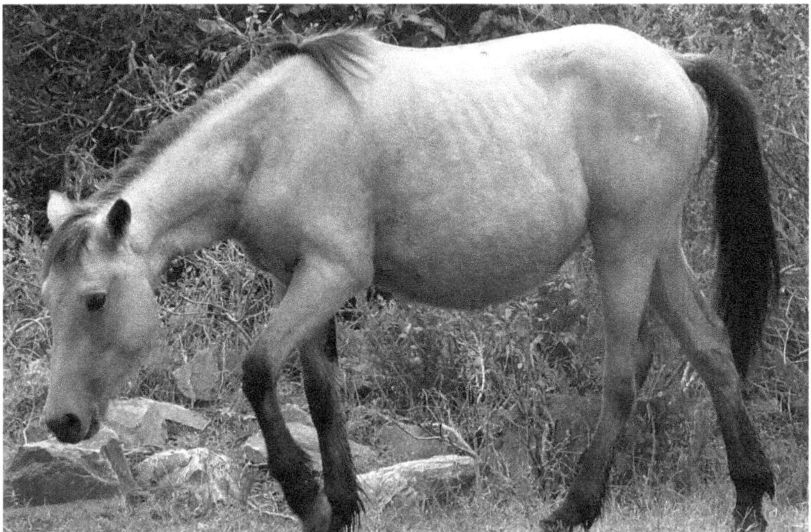

Buckskin

Poco Latte PW

mare   birth year: 2002   brand: 02
GUNNER'S MOON x MISTY DAWN

Brown eyes. Auction price: $6,750. Born July 15, 2002.

Notes:

Poco Latte PW

Sunrise Ocean Tides

Sunny
mare birth year: 2015 brand: 15
Little Dolphin x Jessica's Sea Star Sandy

Brown eyes. Auction price: $3,100. Born May 29, 2015. Buyback donator: Lowrey Family.

Notes:

Sunrise Ocean Tides

Too Grand

Taffee, Salt Water Taffee
mare birth year: 2000 brand: 00
CINNAMON HOLOGRAM X MERRY TEAPOT'S HIGH BID

Brown eyes. Born July 2000. Alternate sire: North Star. Buyback donator: An elementary school class.

Notes:

Too Grand

Kachina Grand Star

Kachina
mare birth year: 2005 brand: 05, partial
NORTH STAR x TOO GRAND

Brown eyes. Auction price: $4,000. Born June 3, 2005. Buyback donator: Ginny Zelevitch and Joanne Rome.

Notes:

Kachina Grand Star

Buckskin Comparison Chart

Name	Pg #	Brand	Mane	Face
Alice's Sandcastle	152	12	right	
Anne Bonny's Little Flower	154	19		
CLG Rider on the Storm	156	19	right	
Ivana Marie Zustan	158	16	right	
Jessica's Sea Star Sandy	160	06	right	
Kachina Grand Star	170	05, partial	left	star
Liz's Serenity	162	17	right	
Poco Latte PW	164	02	right	
Sunrise Ocean Tides	166	15	right	
Too Grand	168	00	left	

NOTES

Left & right refers to the animal's left & right.

Mane: **left** = falls to the left **right** = falls to the right **split** = significant portion falls on left and right

Buckskin Comparison Chart

Legs				
R F	**R B**	**L F**	**L B**	**Notable Details**
				stallion
	sock		sock	
				dark dappled coat

R F = right front **R B** = right back **L F** = left front **L B** = left back
sock = white well below the knee **stocking** = white near and above the knee

baldface = white covers most of the face **blaze** = white streak running down the length of the face **snip** = white spot on the muzzle **star** = white spot on the forehead

Buckskin Pinto

Molly's Rosebud

Rosie
mare   birth year: 2010   brand: none
YANKEE SPIRIT x MERRY TEAPOT'S HIGH BID

Brown eyes. Auction price: $5,800. Born May 4, 2010.

Notes:

Molly's Rosebud

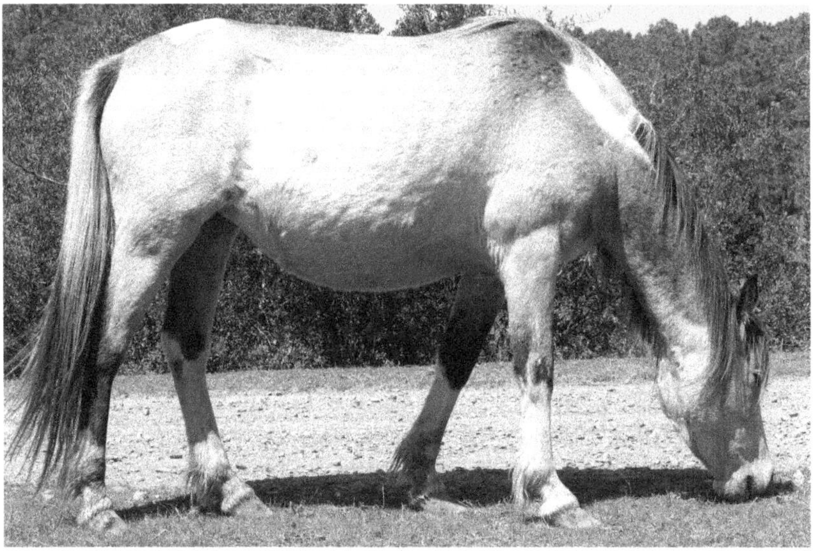

CLG Bay Princess

Bay Princess
mare birth year: 2016 brand: 16
TORNADO'S PRINCE OF TIDES x BAYBE

Brown eyes. Auction price: $10,000. First seen April 22, 2016. Buyback donor: Chincoteague Legacy Group.

Notes:

CLG Bay Princess

CLG ToMorrow's Tidewater Twist

Twist, Triple T, Tidewater Twist
stallion birth year: 2017 brand: 17
TORNADO'S LEGACY x SWEETHEART

Brown eyes. Auction price: $8,400. First seen March 13, 2017. Buyback donor: Chincoteague Legacy Group.

Notes:

CLG ToMorrow's Tidewater Twist

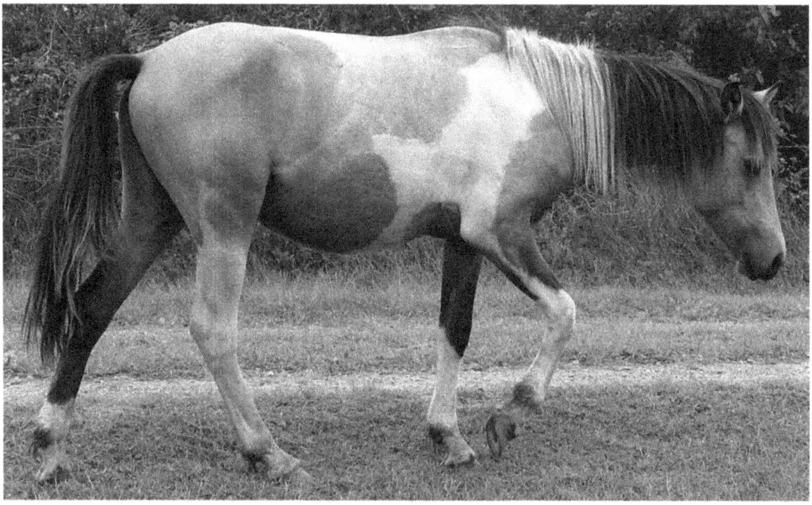

Badabing

mare birth year: 2015 brand: 15
Tornado's Prince of Tides x Ella of Assateague

Brown eyes. Auction price: $4,500. Born May 12, 2015. Buyback donors: Julie Barry, Yuki Banks, and Linda Cook.

Notes:

Badabing

Tornado's Legacy

Legacy, Lil Tornado
stallion birth year: 2007 brand: 07
TORNADO x UNCI

Brown eyes. Auction price: $11,000. Born April 3, 2007.

Notes:

Tornado's Legacy

Buckskin Pinto

Randy

mare birth year: 2014 brand: 14
TORNADO'S PRINCE OF TIDES x BAYBE

Brown eyes. Auction price: $8,100. Buyback donator: Heckman Family.

Notes:

Randy

Buckskin Pinto

Serendipity

mare birth year: 2018 brand: 18
MAVERICK X CALCETÍN

Brown eyes. Auction price: $8,200. Alternate sire: Ace's Black Tie Affair. First seen April 29, 2018. Buyback donator: Gina Marabito Zebley.

Notes:

Serendipity

Tidewater Treasure

Treasure
mare   birth year: 2000   brand: none
CHEROKEE CHIEF x BLONDE

Brown eyes. Donated to CVFC December 2018.

Notes:

Tidewater Treasure

Chestnut

JABATAA

mare birth year: 2002 brand: 02
CHEROKEE CHIEF x ROSIE O' GRADY

Brown eyes. Auction price: $4,900. Born July 2002. Buyback donator: Mauger family.

Notes:

JABATAA

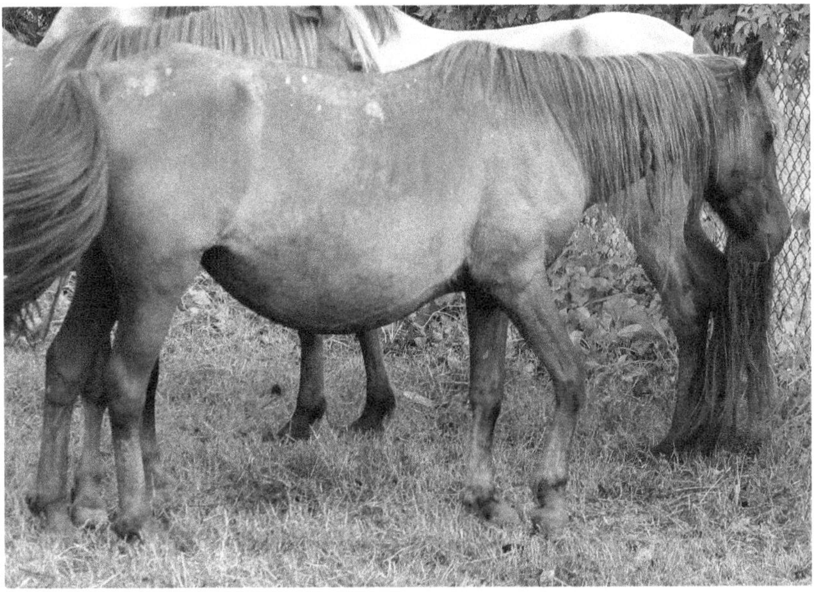

Chestnut

Surfer's Shining Star

Gingersnap
mare birth year: 2015 brand: 15
SURFER DUDE x TSG'S ELUSIVE STAR

Brown eyes. Auction price: $6,500. Born March 23, 2015. Buyback donator: Joyce Westberry.

Notes:

Surfer's Shining Star

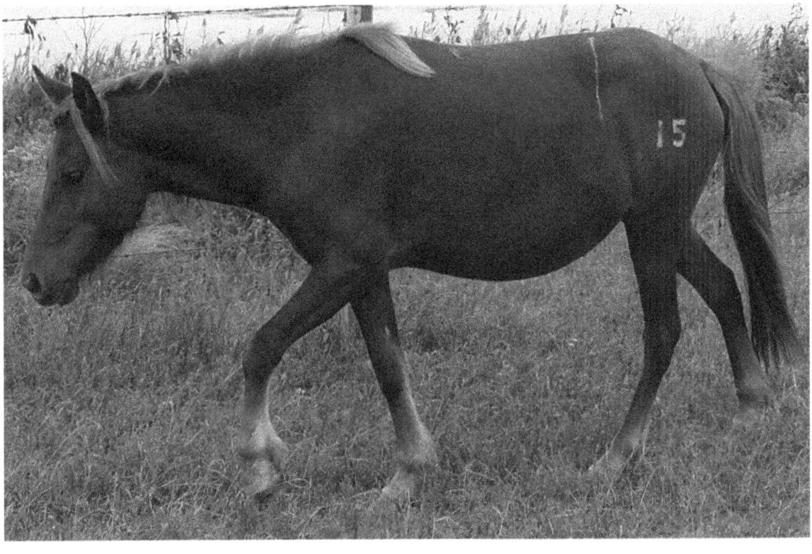

Surfin' Chantel

mare birth year: 2013 brand: 13
RAINBOW WARRIOR x SURFIN' SCARLET

Brown eyes. Born September 2013. Fall buyback.

Notes:

Surfin' Chantel

Susana

mare birth year: 2001 brand: 01
CHEROKEE CHIEF x GLAMOUR GIRL

Brown eyes. Born July 20, 2001. Alternate sire: Surfer Dude. Buyback donator: Strofhoff family.

Notes:

Susana

Chestnut

Suzy's Sweetheart

mare birth year: 1998 brand: 98
CHEROKEE CHIEF X VOYAGER

Brown eyes. Born July 1998. Alternate sire: Tornado.

Notes:

Suzy's Sweetheart

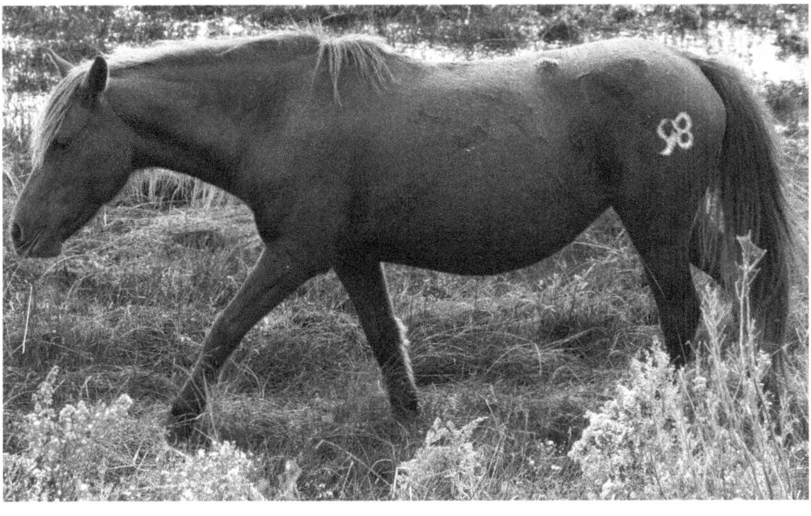

Sue's Crown of Hope

Hope
mare birth year: 2019 brand: 19
KEN X KIMMEE-SUE

Brown eyes. Auction price: $1,600. First seen May 14, 2019. Buyback donor: Joe Lowery, In memory of Sue Wingfield Lowery by family and friends.

Notes:

Sue's Crown of Hope

Surfin' Scarlet

Scarlet
mare birth year: 2000 brand: 00
SURFER DUDE x SURF QUEEN

Brown eyes. Born July 2000. Buyback donator: Strand family.

Notes:

Surfin' Scarlet

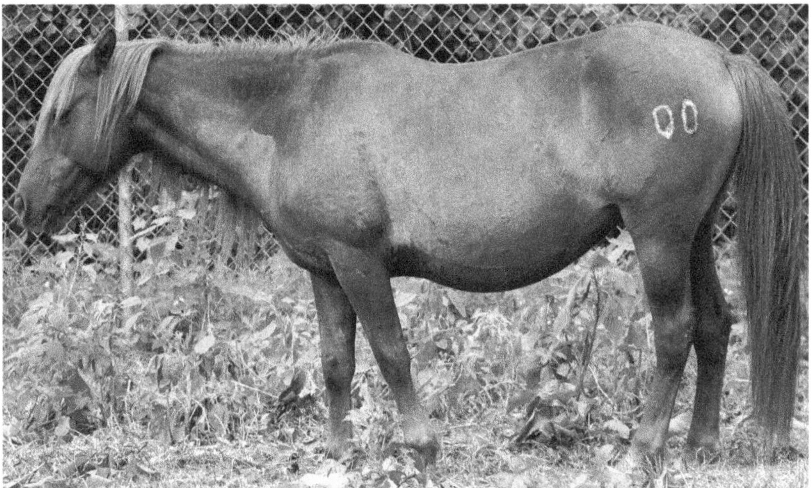

Chestnut

Tuleta Star

mare birth year: 2002 brand: 02
CHEROKEE CHIEF x A TOUCH OF DUST

Brown eyes. Auction price: $5,000. Born July 17, 2002. Buyback donator: Tuleta White.

Notes:

Tuleta Star

Chestnut

Cinnamon Blaze

mare   birth year: 1999   brand: unreadable

(UNKNOWN) x SNEAKERS

Brown eyes.

Notes:

Cinnamon Blaze

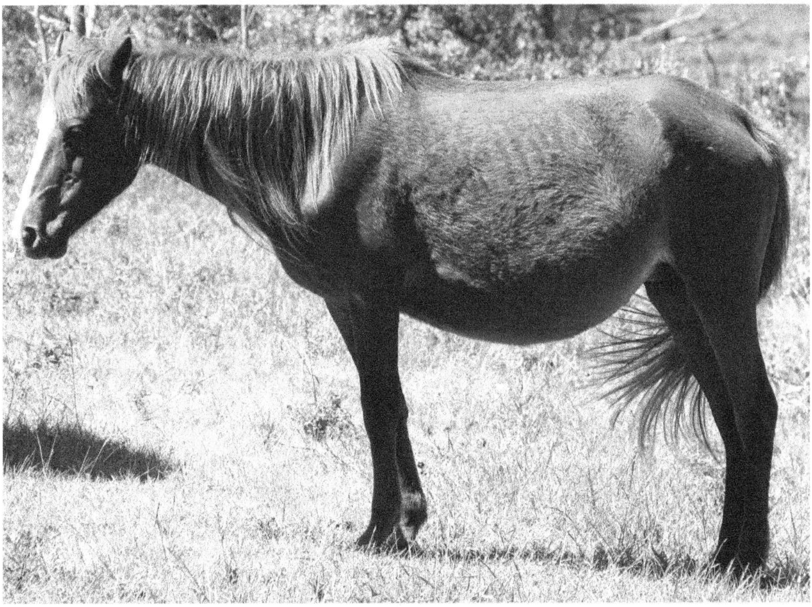

Kimmee-Sue

mare birth year: 2012 brand: 12
Courtney's Boy x Cinnamon Blaze

Brown eyes. Auction price: $5,000. Born May 2, 2012. Buyback donator: Sue Fitzgerald.

Notes:

Kimmee-Sue

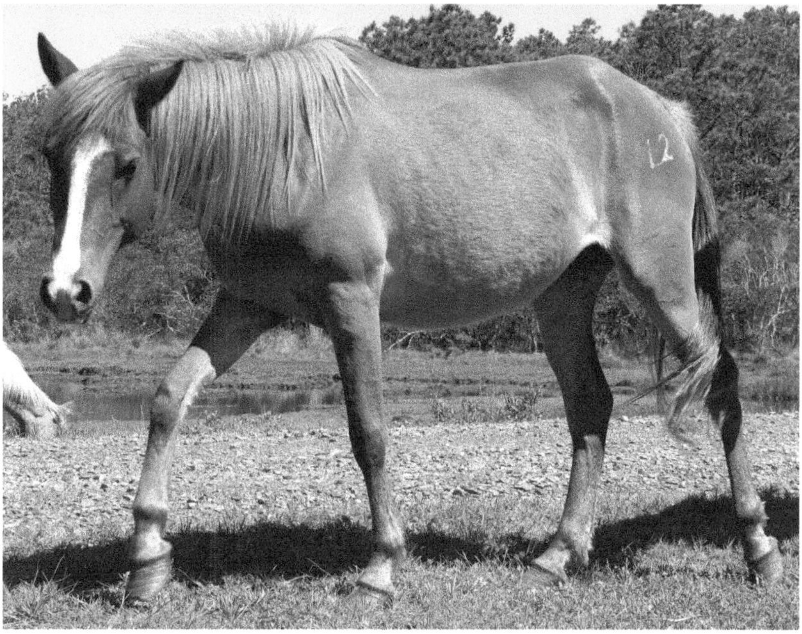

Precious Jewel

mare birth year: 2014 brand: 14
PHANTOM MIST x UNCI

Brown eyes. Auction price: $5,200. Buyback donator: Sibyl and Elton Wright.

Notes:

Precious Jewel

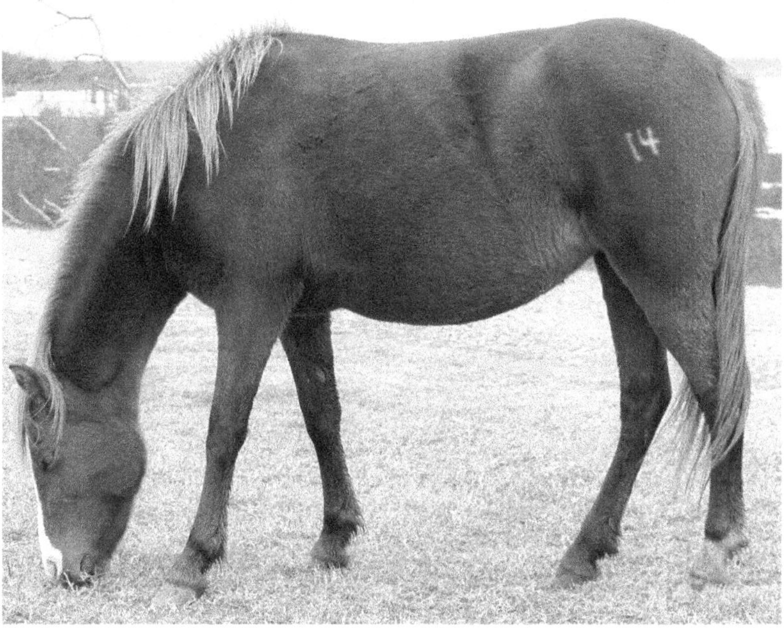

Unforgettable 2001

Diamond
mare birth year: 2001 brand: none
HURRICANE x JUST MY STYLE

Brown eyes. Born September 2001. Alternate dam: Glamour Girl.

Notes:

Unforgettable 2001

Judy's Little Smooch

Smooch
mare birth year: 2016 brand: none
SURFER'S RIPTIDE x BUTTERFLY KISSES

Brown eyes. Born August 9, 2016. Buyback donator: Judy Fuccello.

Notes:

Judy's Little Smooch

Surfer Dude's Gidget

Gidget
mare birth year: 2002 brand: F, 02, partial
SURFER DUDE X VIRGINIA BELLE

Brown eyes. Auction price: $7,800. Born March 12, 2002. Buyback donator: Buyback Babes.

Notes:

Surfer Dude's Gidget

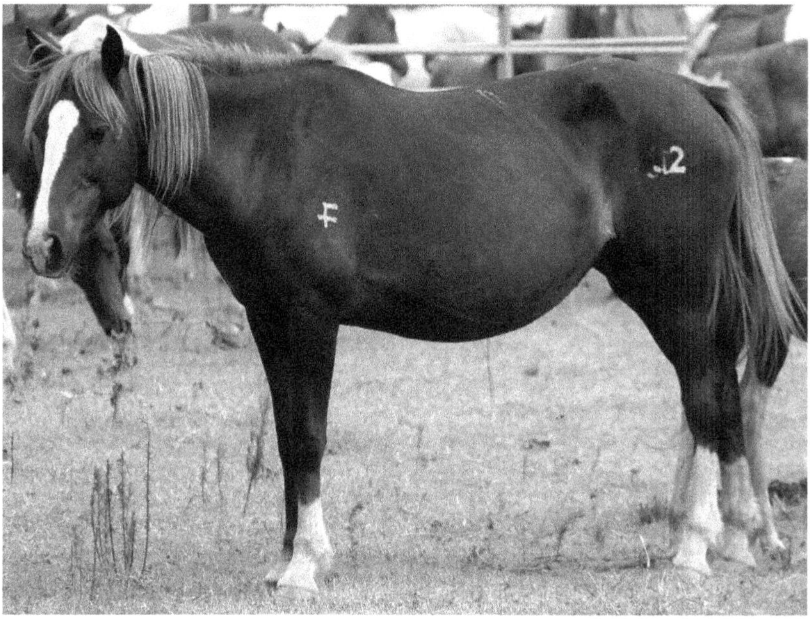

Dreamer's Gift

mare birth year: 2012 brand: 12
SURFER DUDE x LYRA'S VEGA

Brown eyes. Auction price: $4,300. Buyback donor: Janey, Anna, and Amanda Beer. Alternate sire: Surfer's Riptide.

Notes:

Dreamer's Gift

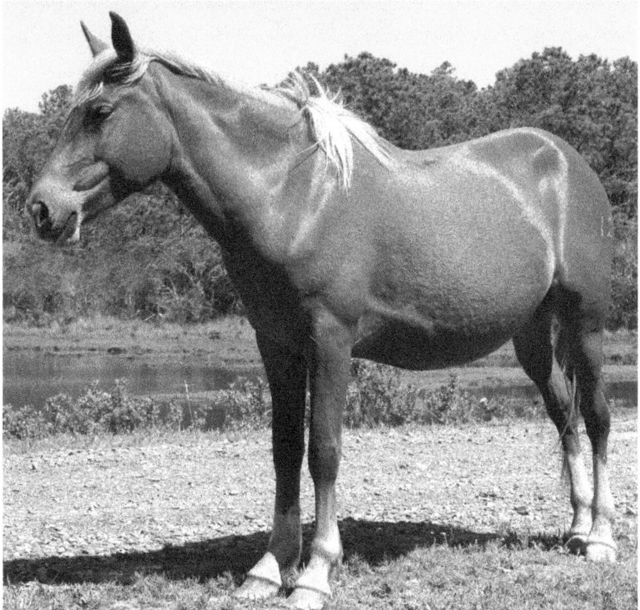

Surfer Princess

mare birth year: 2015 brand: 15

Surfer Dude x Surf Queen

Brown eyes. Auction price: $5,300. Born May 14, 2015. Buyback donators: Julie Barry, Yuki Banks, and Linda Cook.

Notes:

Surfer Princess

Chestnut

Surfette

mare birth year: 2017 brand: 17
WH Salt Marsh x Sundance

Brown eyes. Donated to CVFC March 2018. Great Great Great Great Grandfoal of Misty.

Notes:

Surfette

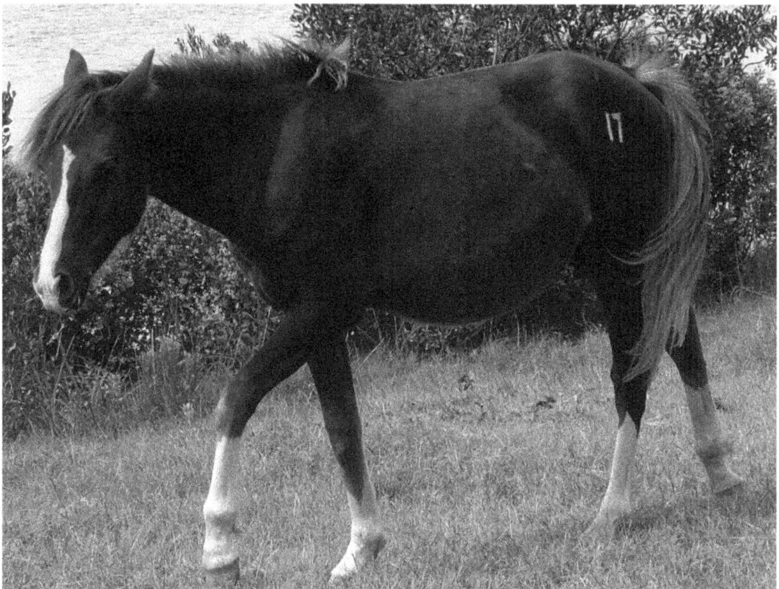

Ken

Valentine
stallion birth year: 2008 brand: 08
WILD THING x STAR GAZER

Brown eyes. Auction price: $4,500. Born February 14, 2008. Alternate sire: Glacier. Buyback donator: Sue Lowery.

Notes:

Ken

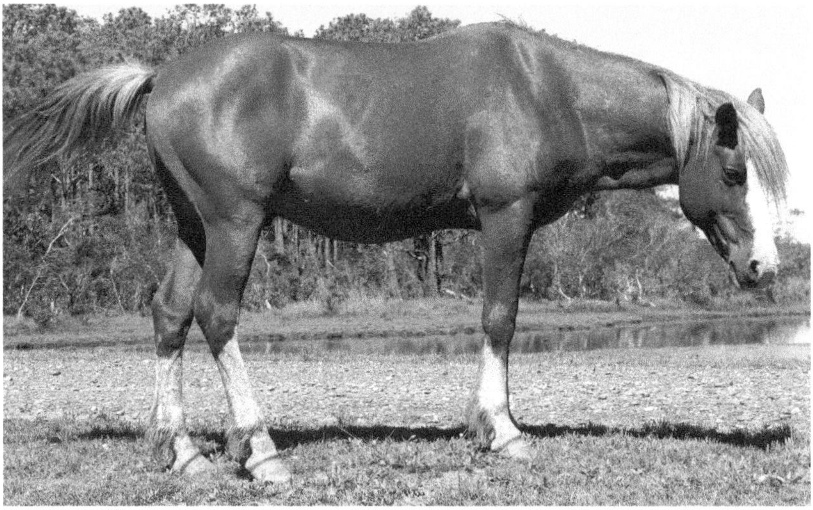

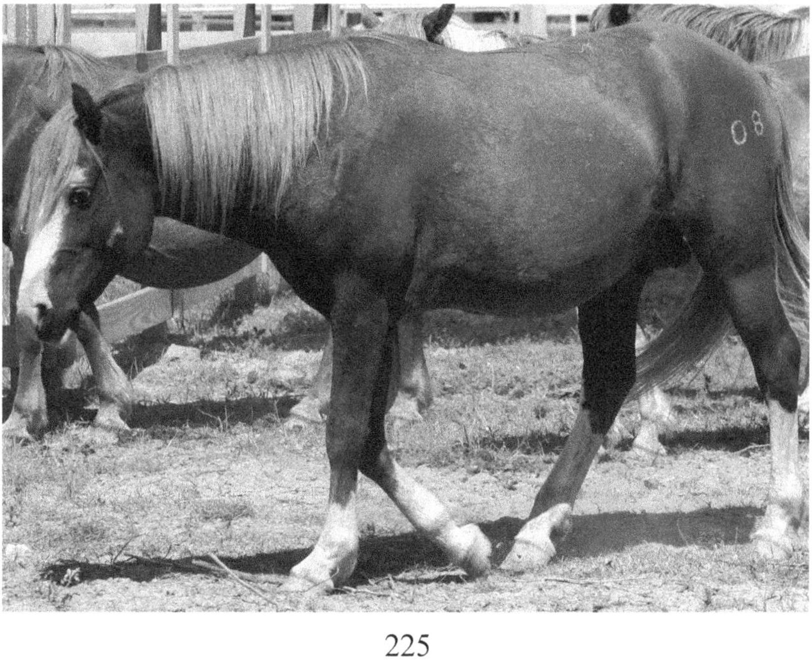

Dreamer's Stardust

Stardust
mare birth year: 2018 brand: 18
KEN X DREAMER'S GIFT

Brown eyes. First seen March 8, 2018. Buyback donor: Beer Family.

Notes:

Dreamer's Stardust

Chestnut

Surfer's Riptide

Riptide, Rip Tide
stallion birth year: 2009 brand: 09, partial
SURFER DUDE X SURF QUEEN

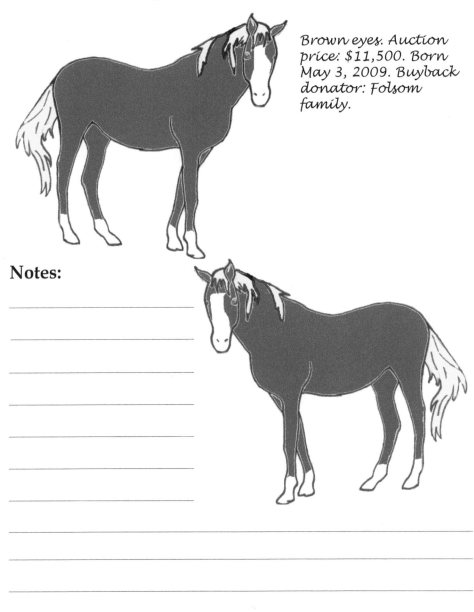

Brown eyes. Auction price: $11,500. Born May 3, 2009. Buyback donator: Folsom family.

Notes:

Surfer's Riptide

Chestnut Comparison Chart

Name	Pg #	Brand	Mane	Face
Cinnamon Blaze	206	unreadable	left	blaze
Dreamer's Gift	218	12	split	star and snip
Dreamer's Stardust	226	18	split	blaze
JABATAA	190	02	right	
Judy's Little Smooch	214		right	blaze
Ken	224	08	left	baldface
Kimmee-Sue	208	12	left	blaze
Precious Jewel	210	14	split	blaze
Sue's Crown of Hope	200	19	right	star
Surfer Dude's Gidget	216	F, 02, partial	split	blaze
Surfer Princess	220	15	right	star and snip
Surfer's Riptide	228	09, partial	right	baldface
Surfer's Shining Star	192	15	right	
Surfette	222	17	right	blaze
Surfin' Chantel	194	13	right	
Surfin' Scarlet	202	00	right	star
Susana	196	01	right	
Suzy's Sweetheart	198	98	right	
Tuleta Star	204	02	right	star and snip
Unforgettable 2001	212		left	star

NOTES

Left & right refers to the animal's left & right.

Mane: **left** = falls to the left **right** = falls to the right **split** = significant portion falls on left and right

R F = right front **R B** = right back **L F** = left front **L B** = left back
sock = white well below the knee **stocking** = white near and above the knee

Legs				
R F	R B	L F	L B	Notable Details
sock	sock	sock	sock	blond mane & tail
stocking	stocking	stocking	stocking	blond mane & tail
				very dark coat
	stocking			
sock	stocking	sock	stocking	stallion; small white kiss mark on left cheek; blond mane & tail
			sock	
				large crescent shaped star; 1 in brand is smeared
	sock	sock	sock	dark coat; much lighter mane & tail
sock	sock	sock	sock	arrowhead shaped spot on left side
stocking	stocking	stocking	stocking	stallion; dark coat; blond mane & tail; long forelock covers eyes
				dark red coat; mane & tail a little lighter
sock	sock	sock	sock	dark brown
				small whitish diamond-shaped patch on right hip
				small stature
				long forelock
		sock	sock	dark coat

baldface = white covers most of the face **blaze** = white streak running down the length of the face **snip** = white spot on the muzzle **star** = white spot on the forehead

Catwalk's Olympic Glory

Glory
mare birth year: 2016 brand: 16
AJAX X CATWALK CHAOS

Brown eyes. Auction price: $8,100. Born May 2, 2016. Buyback donor: Leslie Joliet.

Notes:

Catwalk's Olympic Glory

Chestnut Pinto

Chili

Lil Miss Hot Stuff
mare birth year: 2016 brand: 17, partial
CHIEF GOLDEN EAGLE X CLOUDBURST

Brown eyes. Born September 24, 2016. Donated to CVFC March 2018.

Notes:

Chili

Chestnut Pinto

Slash of White

mare birth year: 1998 brand: 98
WITCH DOCTOR x SWEET MISCHIEF

Brown eyes. Born July 1998.

Notes:

Slash of White

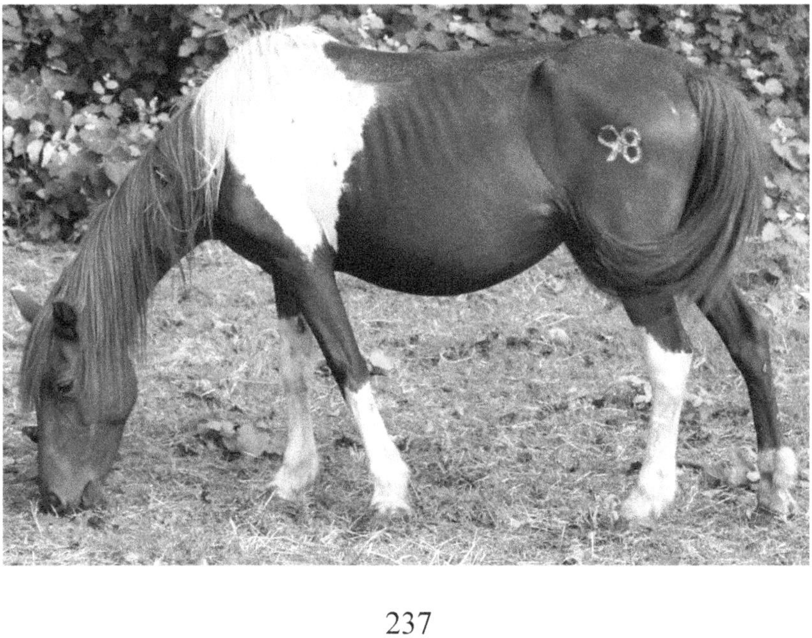

Lefty's Checkmark

Butterfly
mare birth year: 2000 brand: none
CHEROKEE CHIEF X RAPT IN PAINT

Brown eyes.

Notes:

Lefty's Checkmark

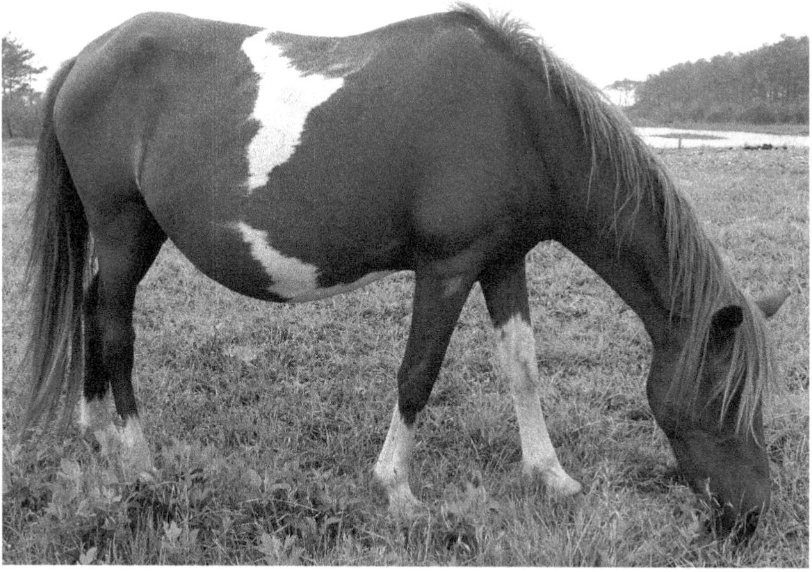

Chestnut Pinto

CJ SAMM'N

mare birth year: 2006 brand: 06

NORTH STAR X SLASH OF WHITE

Brown eyes. Auction price: $3,700. Born May 7, 2006. Alternate sire: Leonard Stud.

Notes:

CJ SAMM'N

Chestnut Pinto

Kimball's Rainbow Delight

Rainy, Rainbow Delight
mare birth year: 2006 brand: 06, partial
North Star x Rambling Ruby

Brown eyes. Auction price: $3,100. Born May 9, 2006. Buyback donator: Mary and Normal Kimball.

Notes:

Kimball's Rainbow Delight

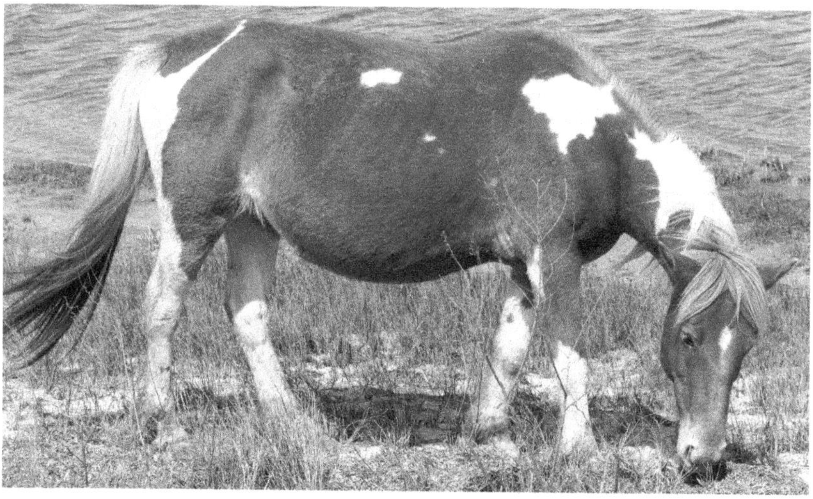

Chestnut Pinto

Good Ole Days Bailey's Star

Star
mare birth year: 2004 brand: none
(UNKNOWN) X (UNKNOWN)

Brown eyes. Donated to CVFC December 2018.

Notes:

Good Ole Days Bailey's Star

Chestnut Pinto

Tiger Lily

Waterbaby
mare birth year: 2002 brand: none
CHEROKEE CHIEF X VOYAGER

Brown eyes. Born September 2002.

Notes:

Tiger Lily

Pony Girl's Bliss

Bliss
mare birth year: 2017 brand: 17
Effie's Papa Bear x Carol's Little Freedom

Brown eyes. Auction price: $7,100. First seen June 4, 2017. Buyback donor: Cassou family.

Notes:

Pony Girl's Bliss

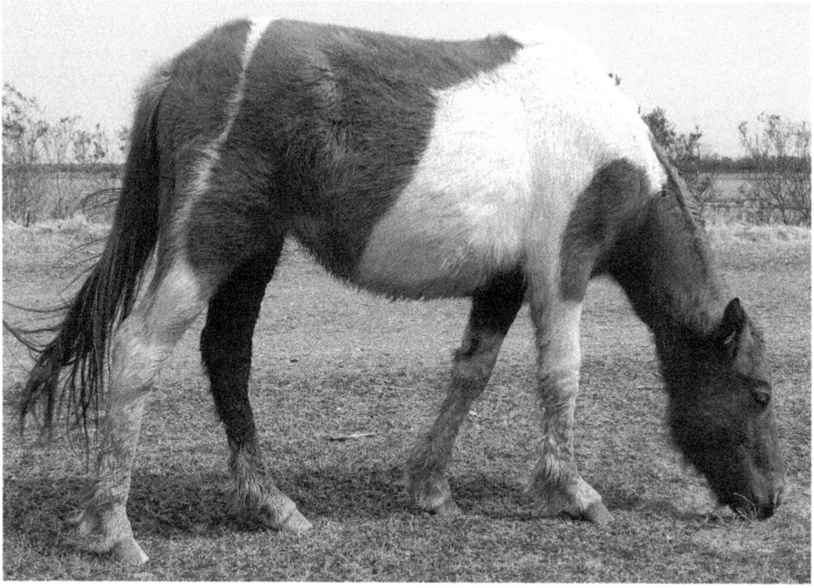

Susie Q

Lady Hook
mare birth year: 1996 brand: 96
PREMIERRE x VIXEN

Brown eyes. Auction price: $3,600. Born May 1996.

Notes:

Susie Q

Catwalk Chaos

Margarita
mare birth year: 2010 brand: none
CHAOS X PAINT BY NUMBER

Brown eyes. Auction price: $8,100. Born May 8, 2010.

Notes:

Catwalk Chaos

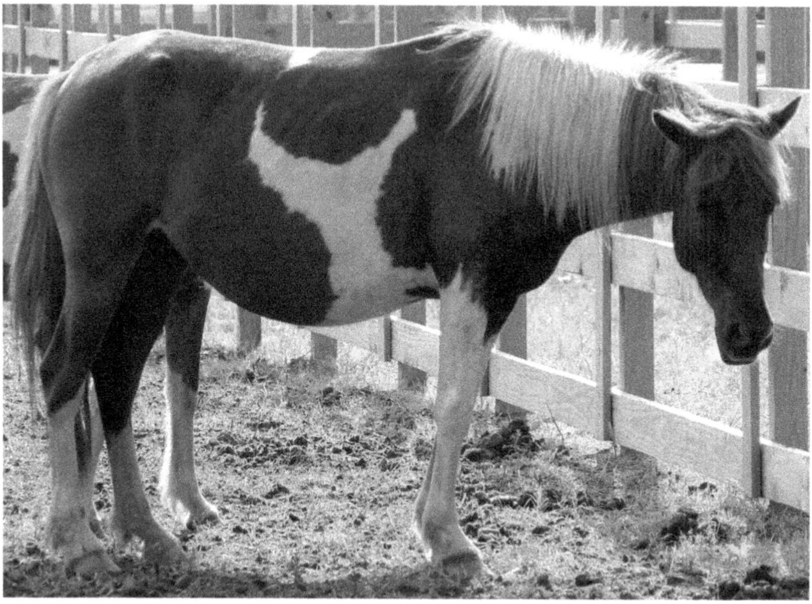

Chestnut Pinto

Carli Marie

mare birth year: 2018 brand: 18

ACE'S BLACK TIE AFFAIR x GIDGET'S BEACH BABY

Brown eyes. Auction price: $7,000. First seen April 29, 2018.

Notes:

Carli Marie

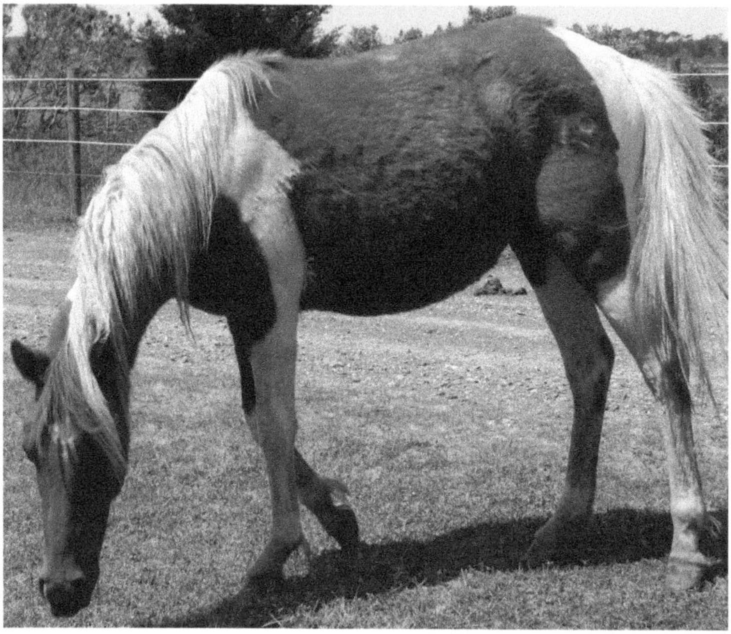

Chestnut Pinto

Anne Bonny

mare birth year: 2012 brand: none
YANKEE SPIRIT x MYSTERY

Brown eyes. Auction price: $4,200. Born April 25, 2011. Buyback donor: Sarah Sickles.

Notes:

Anne Bonny

Chestnut Pinto

Sweet Jane

Duckie
mare birth year: 2006 brand: 06, partial
COURTNEY'S BOY X LEFTY'S CHECKMARK

Brown eyes. Auction price: $4,200. Born April 6, 2006. Buyback donor: Sara Rasmussen.

Notes:

Sweet Jane

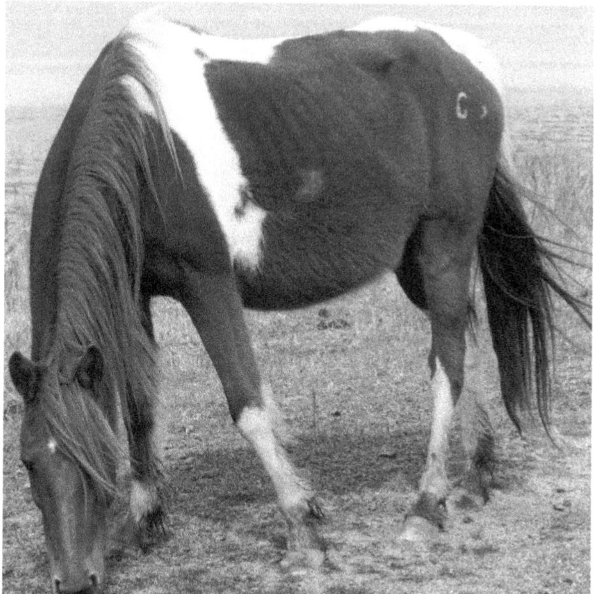

Chestnut Pinto

Little Duckie

Quackers
mare birth year: 2011 brand: F
NORTH STAR x SWEET JANE

Brown eyes. Auction price: $3,200. Born May 28, 2011.

Notes:

Little Duckie

Chestnut Pinto

Two Teagues Taco's Chilibean

Chilibean
mare birth year: 2019 brand: 19
ACE'S BLACK TIE AFFAIR x TWO TEAGUES TACO

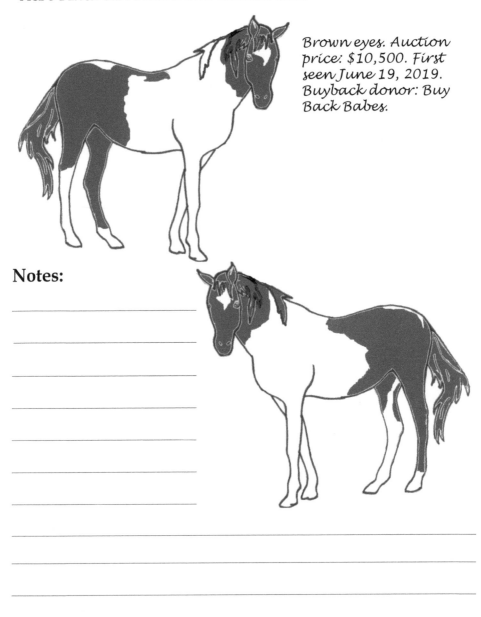

Brown eyes. Auction price: $10,500. First seen June 19, 2019. Buyback donor: Buy Back Babes.

Notes:

Two Teagues Taco's Chilibean

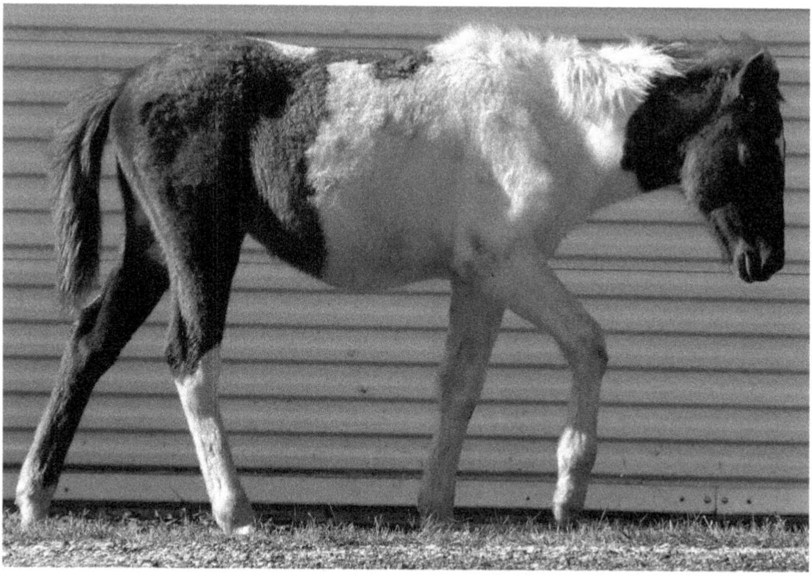

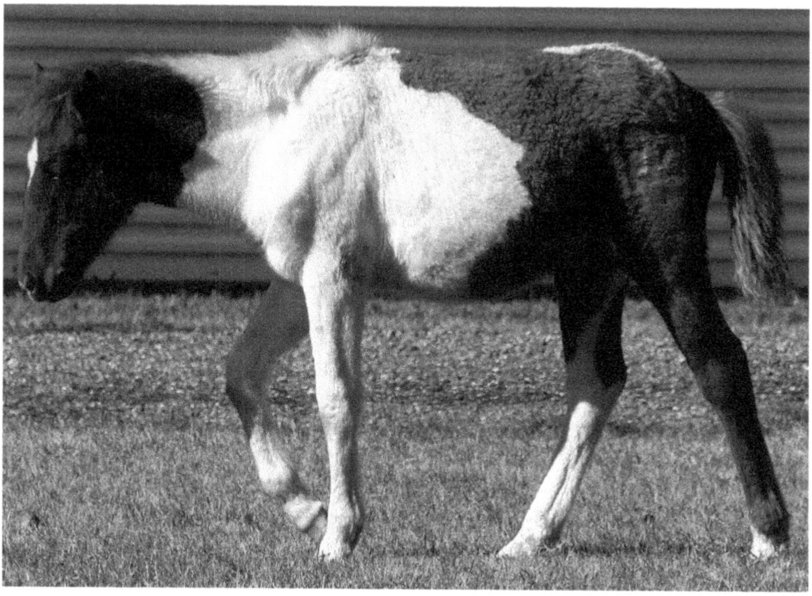

Chestnut Pinto

Misty Mills

mare birth year: 2006 brand: 06, partial
COURTNEY'S BOY x SWEET MISCHIEF

Brown eyes. Auction price: $5,000. Born June 20, 2006.

Notes:

Misty Mills

Chestnut Pinto

Beach Bunny

mare birth year: 2015 brand: 15
ARCHER'S GAMBIT x SWEET JANE

Brown eyes. Auction price: $6,000. Born May 13, 2015.

Notes:

Beach Bunny

Archer's Gambit

Puzzle, Little Frog
stallion   birth year: 2008   brand: 08
NORTH STAR x LILY PAD

Brown eyes. Auction price: $5,300. Born April 24, 2008.

Notes:

Archer's Gambit

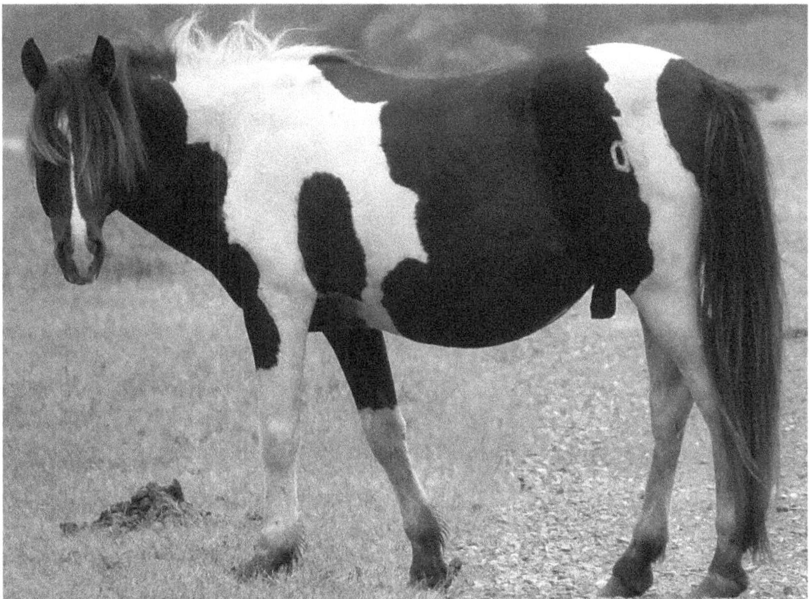

Checkers

Giraffe
mare birth year: 1997 brand: 7, partial
(UNKNOWN) x HITCH HIKER

Brown eyes. Born August 1997. Buyback donator: Fitzgerald family.

Notes:

Checkers

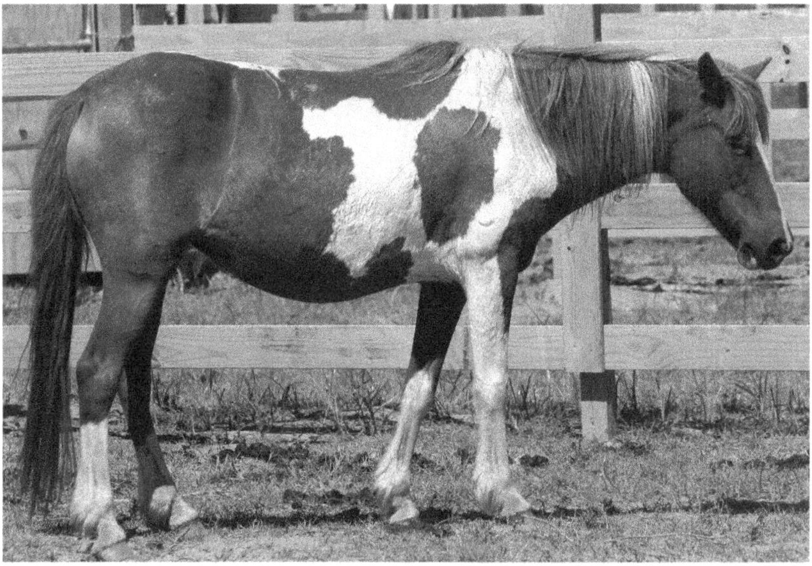

Chestnut Pinto

Stevenson's Dakota Sky

Dakota, Dakota Sky
mare birth year: 2001 brand: 01
COURTNEY'S BOY X PROMISE OF SUMMER

Brown eyes. Born July 17, 2001. Buyback donator: Catherine Young.

Notes:

Stevenson's Dakota Sky

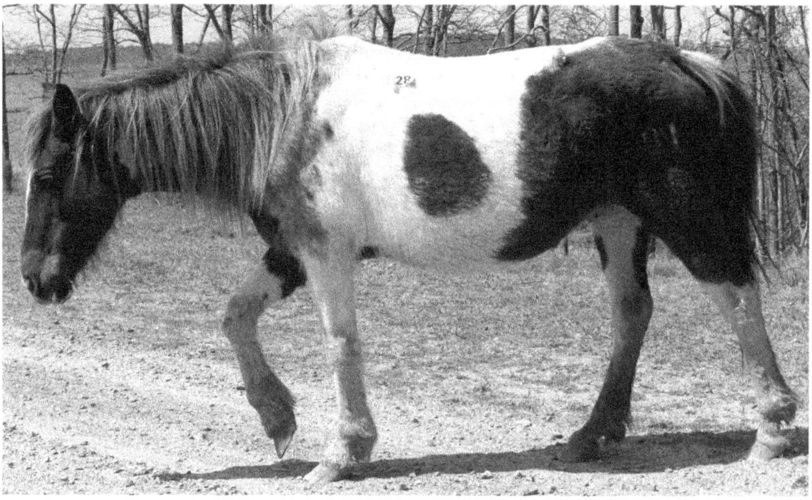

Myrt & Brenda's Indiana Girl

Indy, Indiana Girl
mare birth year: 2020 brand: 20
MAVERICK x FIFTEEN FRIENDS OF FRECKLES

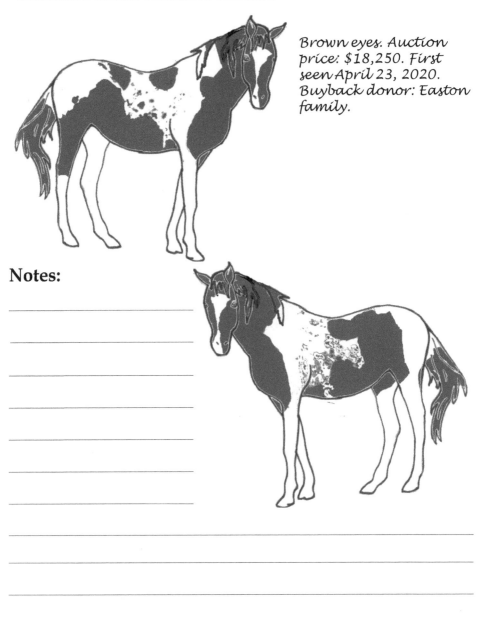

Brown eyes. Auction price: $18,250. First seen April 23, 2020. Buyback donor: Easton family.

Notes:

Myrt & Brenda's Indiana Girl

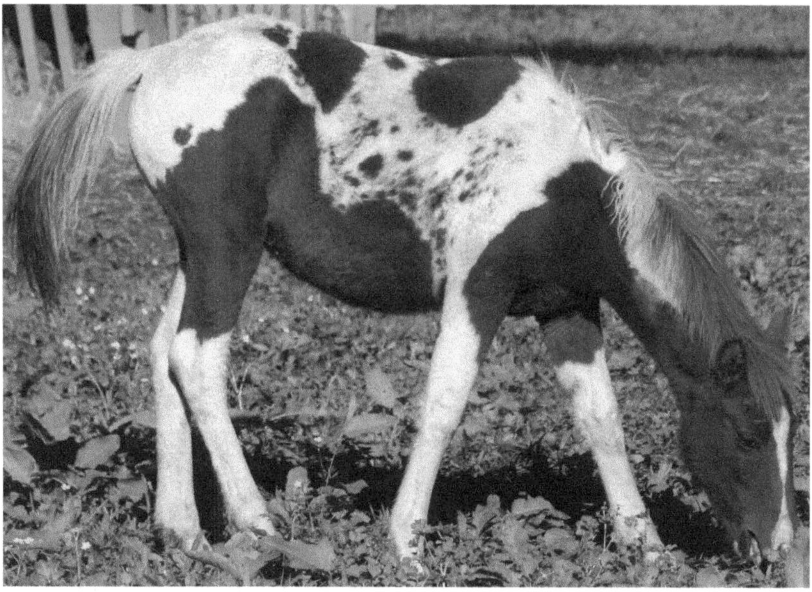

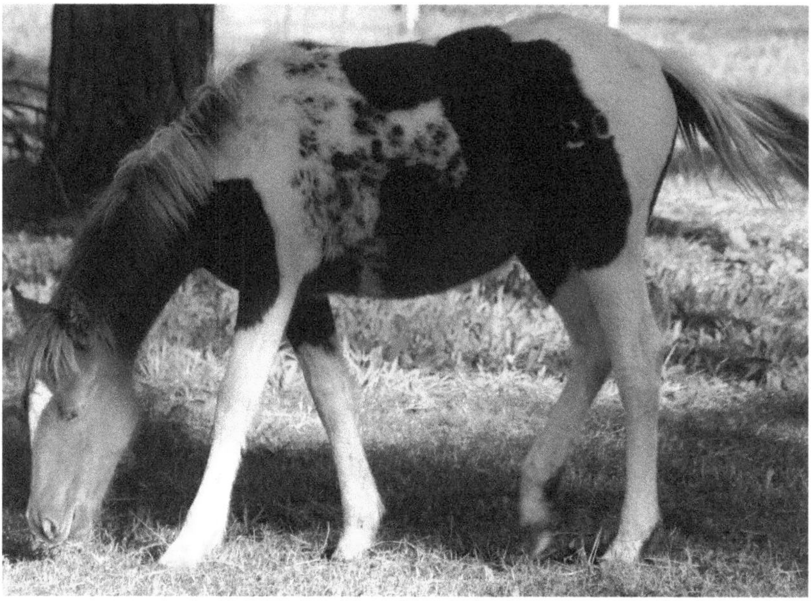

Chestnut Pinto

Sunny Skies After The Storm

Sunny Skies
mare birth year: 2019 brand: 19
ARCHER'S GAMBIT x THUNDERSTORM SKIES

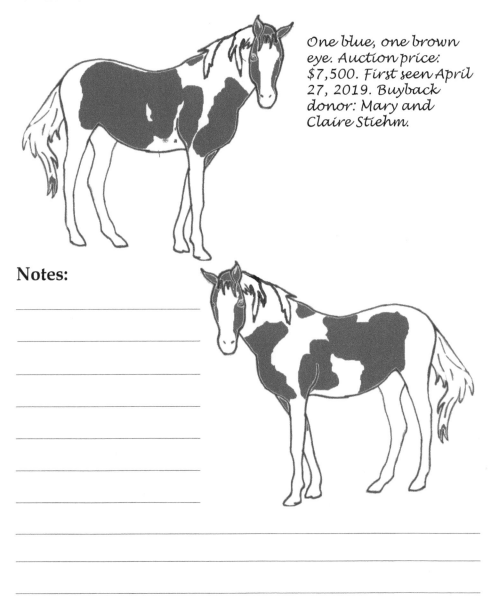

One blue, one brown eye. Auction price: $7,500. First seen April 27, 2019. Buyback donor: Mary and Claire Stiehm.

Notes:

Sunny Skies After The Storm

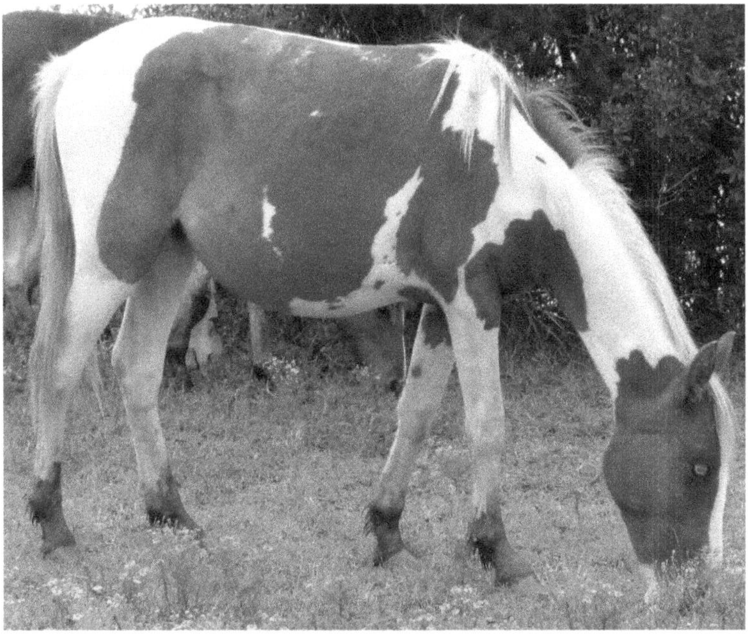

Clara's Glory

Clara
mare birth year: 2020 brand: 20
TORNADO'S LEGACY X CATWALK'S OLYMPIC GLORY

Brown eyes. Auction price: $15,500. First seen June 18, 2020.

Notes:

Clara's Glory

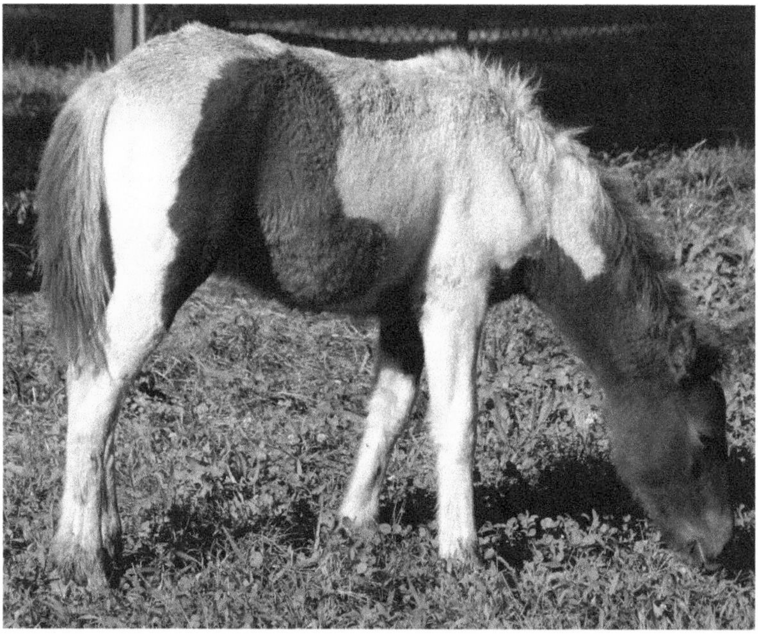

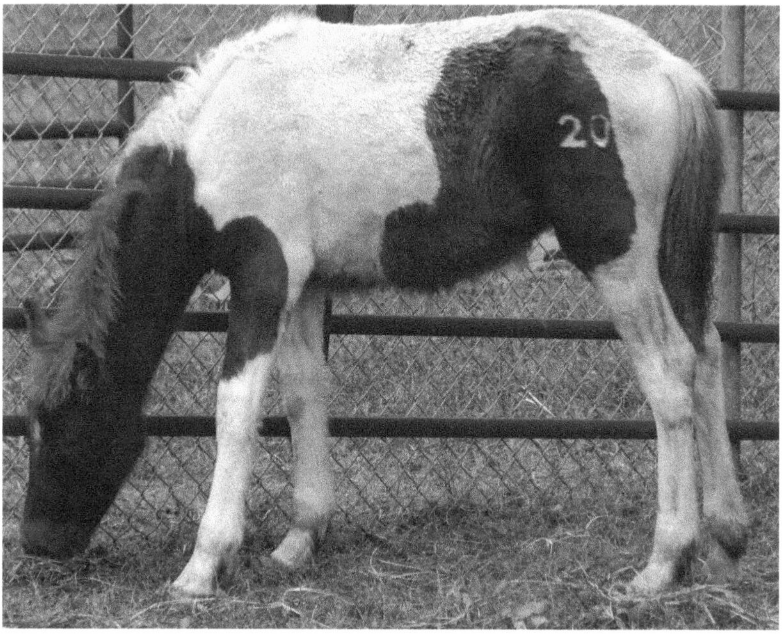

Courtney's Island Dove

Dove
mare birth year: 2006 brand: unreadable
COURTNEY'S BOY x SALT AND PEPPER

Brown eyes. Auction price: $2,300. Buyback donor: Joann Rome and Ginny Zlevitch.

Notes:

Courtney's Island Dove

Chestnut Pinto

Little Bit O' Joansie

Joansie
mare birth year: 2014 brand: 14
COURTNEY'S BOY X CINNAMON BLAZE

Brown eyes. Auction price: $7,100.

Notes:

Little Bit O' Joansie

Chestnut Pinto

Cher's Hope

Cher

mare birth year: 2020 brand: 20

TORNADO'S PRINCE OF TIDES X CATWALK CHAOS

Brown eyes. Auction price: $20,250. First seen March 29, 2020. Buyback donor: Cheryl Kornegay.

Notes:

Cher's Hope

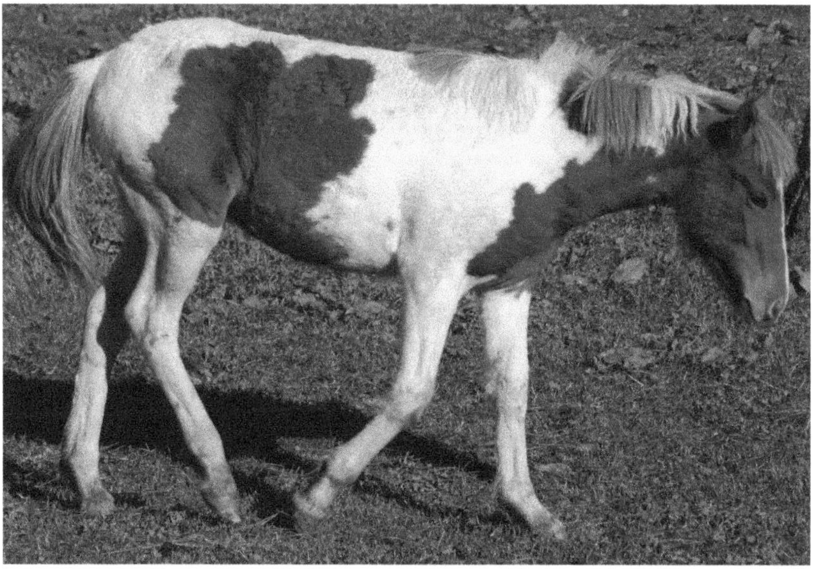

Don Leonard Stud II

Lenny, Leonard Stud II
stallion birth year: 2014 brand: 14
PHANTOM MIST X TUNIE

Brown eyes. Auction price: $9,000. Buyback donor: Leonard Family.

Notes:

Don Leonard Stud II

Chestnut Pinto

Mary Read

mare birth year: 2017 brand: 17

TORNADO'S LEGACY X ANNE BONNY

Brown eyes. Auction price: $7,500. First seen March 5, 2017. Buyback donator: Darcy Cole, Allison Dotzel, and Sarah Sickles.

Notes:

Mary Read

Thetis

mare birth year: 2001 brand: 01
Hot Air Balloon x Untouchable

Brown eyes. Born July 19, 2001. Alternate sire: Courtney's Boy.

Notes:

Thetis

Chestnut Pinto

Sonny's Legacy

mare birth year: 2013 brand: 13
DON LEONARD STUD X SHY ANNE

Brown eyes. Born May 10, 2013. Not auctioned, donated in memory of fireman Sonny Haigh.

Notes:

Chestnut Pinto

Sonny's Legacy

Gidget's Beach Baby

Beach Baby
mare birth year: 2010 brand: none
North Star x Surfer Dude's Gidget

Brown eyes. Auction price: $5,500. Born May 13, 2010. Buyback donator: Buyback Babes.

Notes:

Gidget's Beach Baby

Chestnut Pinto

Wildfire

mare birth year: 2013 brand: none
WH Nightwind x WH Sea Breeze

Brown eyes. Donated to CVFC March 2018. Great Great Great Grandfoal of Misty.

Notes:

Wildfire

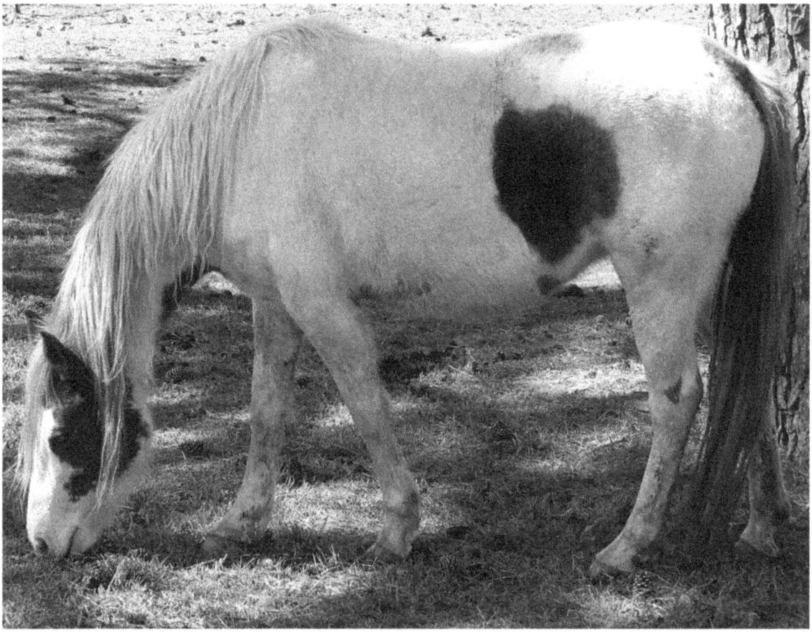

Casade's Fancy Pants

Fancy Pants
mare birth year: 2020 brand: 20
SURFER'S RIPTIDE x POCO'S STARRY NIGHT

Brown eyes. Auction price: $11,500. First seen May 16, 2020. Buyback donor: Toni Cox.

Notes:

Casade's Fancy Pants

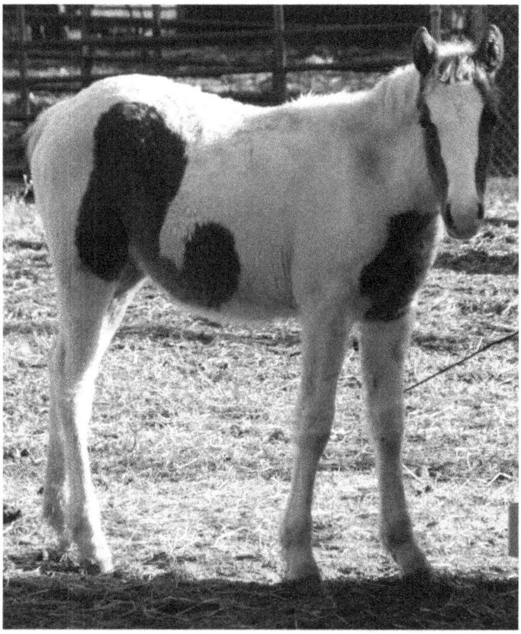

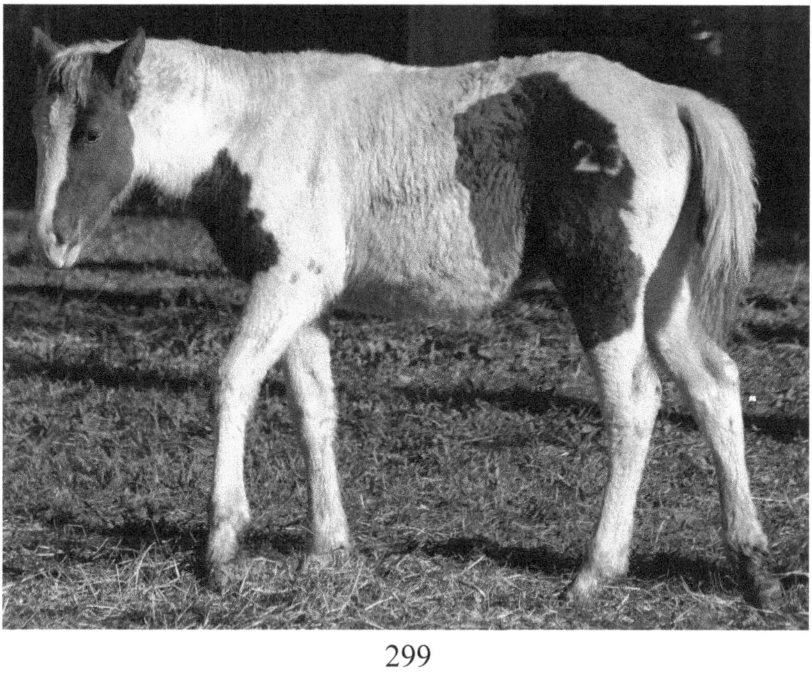

Thunderstorm Skies

Thunder
mare birth year: 2013 brand: 13
DON LEONARD STUD x LILY PAD

Brown eyes. Auction price: $4,000. Born May 7, 2013. Buyback donator: Laura and George De Berdt Romilly.

Notes:

Thunderstorm Skies

CLG Rumor Has It

Rumor
mare birth year: 2018 brand: 18
KEN x WHISPER OF LIVING LEGEND

One blue eye, one brown eye. Auction price: $13,200. First seen May 9, 2018. Buyback donor: Chincoteague Legacy Group.

Notes:

CLG Rumor Has It

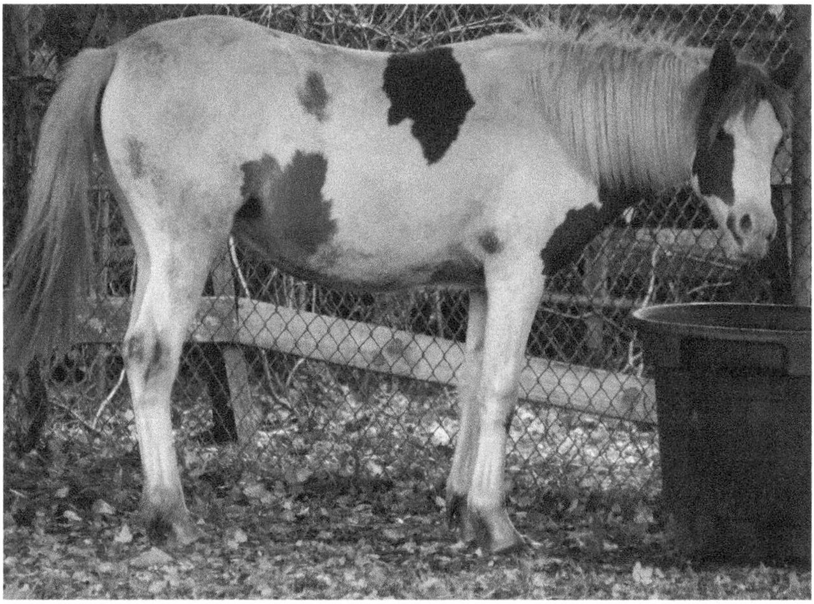

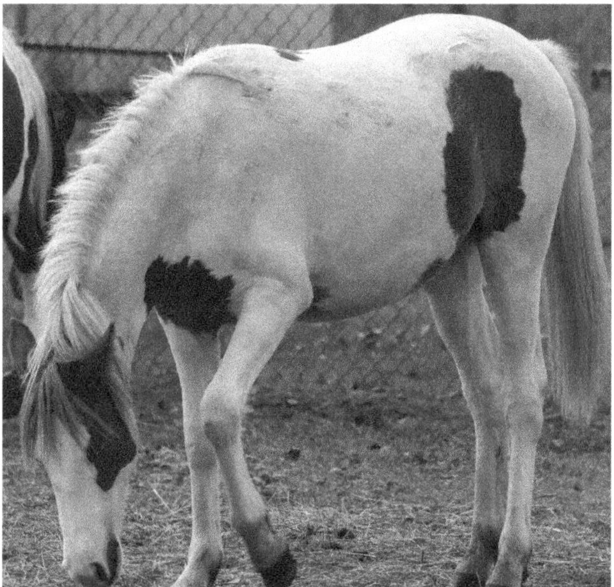

Chestnut Pinto

Delilah's Sandpiper

Piper
mare birth year: 2020 brand: 20
CLG ToMorrow's Tidewater Twist x MissMe

Brown eyes. Auction price: $14,800. First seen May 21, 2020. Buyback donor: Judy Fuccello.

Notes:

Delilah's Sandpiper

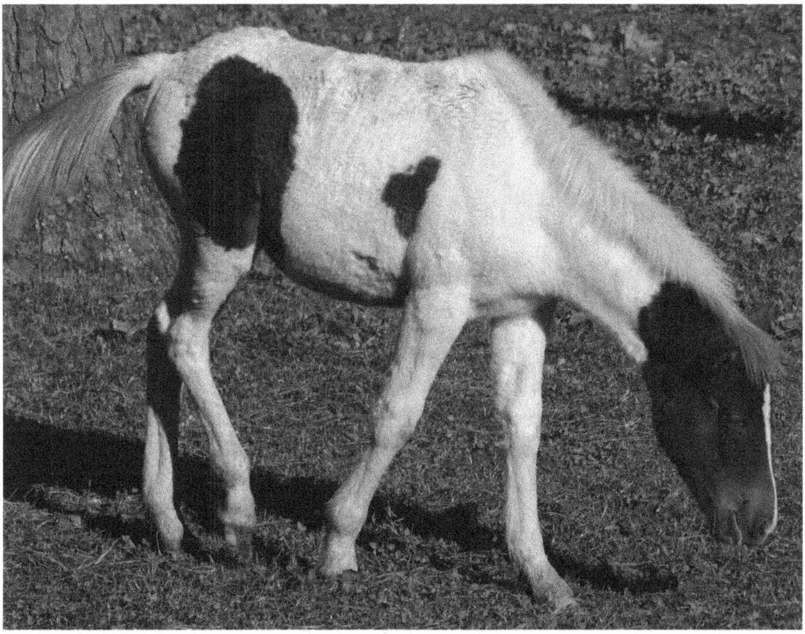

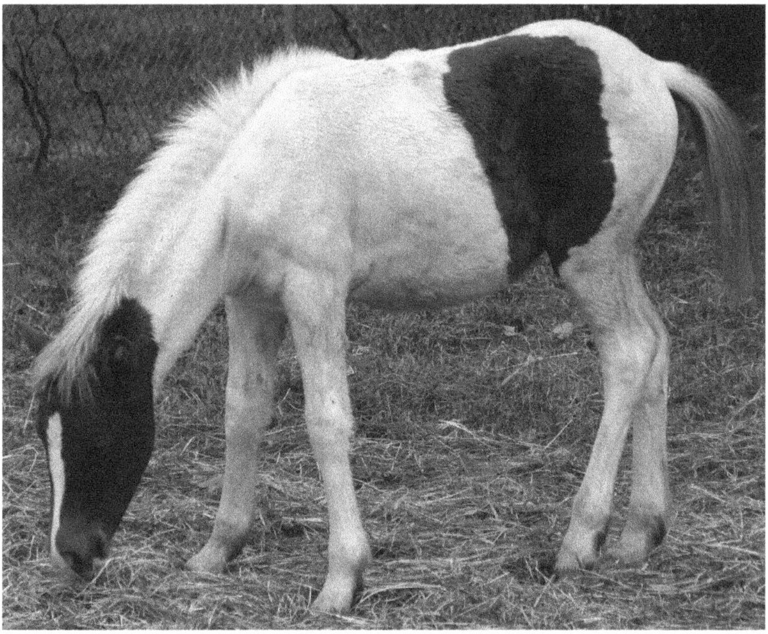

Palomino

Chief Golden Eagle

Chief
stallion birth year: 2008 brand: 08
GLACIER x BEAUTIFUL DREAMER

Brown eyes. Auction price: $3,800. Born April 1, 2008. Buyback donor: Joann Rome and Ginny Zlevitch.

Notes:

Chief Golden Eagle

Kachina Mayli Mist

Mayli
mare birth year: 2012 brand: 12
Phantom Mist x Kachina Grand Star

Brown eyes. Auction price: $7,000. Born April 3, 2012. Buyback donator: Joanne Rome, Ginny Zelevitch, Lowery Family.

Notes:

Kachina Mayli Mist

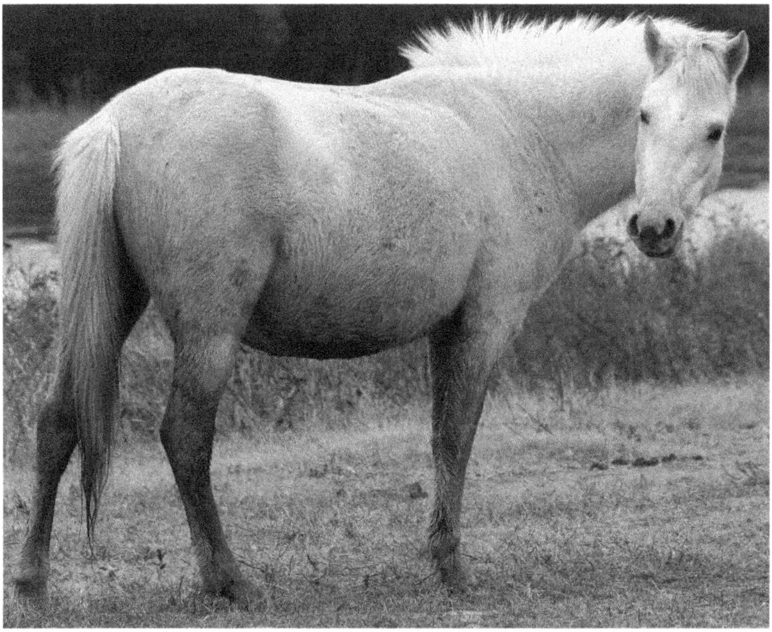

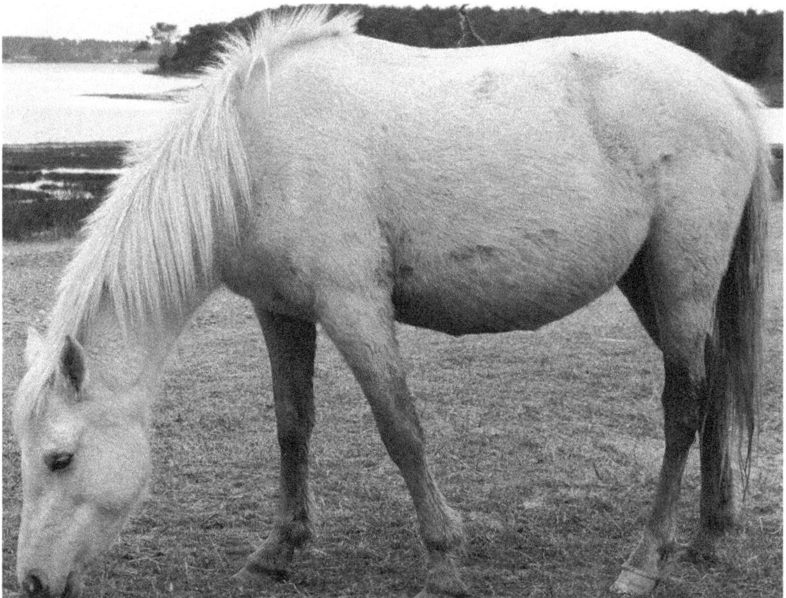

Shy & Sassy Sweet Lady Suede

Suede
mare   birth year: 2014   brand: 14
CHIEF GOLDEN EAGLE x PONY LADIES' SWEET SURPRISE

Brown eyes. Auction price: $7,000. Buyback donator: Kim Theriault.

Notes:

Shy & Sassy Sweet Lady Suede

Two Teague's Golden Girl

Goldie
mare birth year: 2016 brand: 16
CHIEF GOLDEN EAGLE x TWO TEAGUES TACO

Brown eyes. Auction price: $5,000. First seen May 14, 2016. Buyback donator: Buyback Babes.

Notes:

Two Teague's Golden Girl

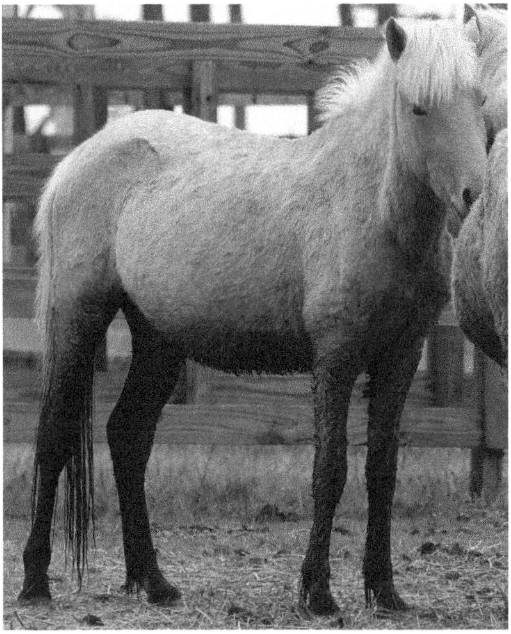

Miss Admiral Halsey

mare birth year: 2018 brand: 18
SURFER'S RIPTIDE x KACHINA MAYLI MIST

Brown eyes. Auction price: $10,200. First seen May 1, 2018. Buyback donator: Meredith Wright.

Notes:

Miss Admiral Halsey

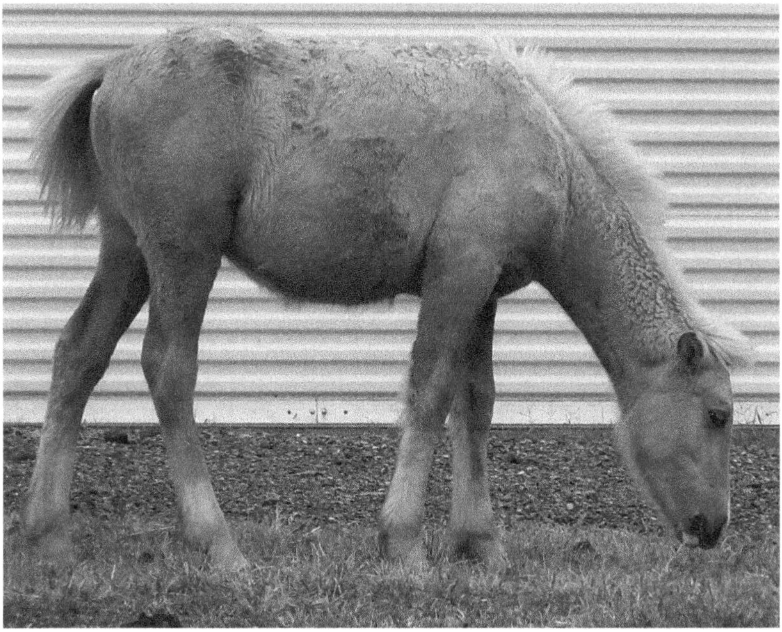

Palomino Comparison Chart

Name	Pg #	Brand	Mane	Face
Chief Golden Eagle	306	08	left	
Kachina Mayli Mist	308	12	left	
Miss Admiral Halsey	314	18	left	blaze
Shy & Sassy Sweet Lady Suede	310	14	split	
Two Teague's Golden Girl	312	16	left	

NOTES

Left & right refers to the animal's left & right.

Mane: **left** = falls to the left **right** = falls to the right **split** = significant portion falls on left and right

Palomino Comparison Chart

Legs				
R F	**R B**	**L F**	**L B**	**Notable Details**
				stallion; long forelock
				pale coat; short hairs stand up along neck like a mohawk
sock	sock	sock	sock	only one with white on face and legs

R F = right front **R B** = right back **L F** = left front **L B** = left back
sock = white well below the knee **stocking** = white near and above the knee

baldface = white covers most of the face **blaze** = white streak running down the length of the face **snip** = white spot on the muzzle **star** = white spot on the forehead

Judy's Sunshine

Wings
mare birth year: 2018 brand: 18
TORNADO'S PRINCE OF TIDES x CATWALK CHAOS

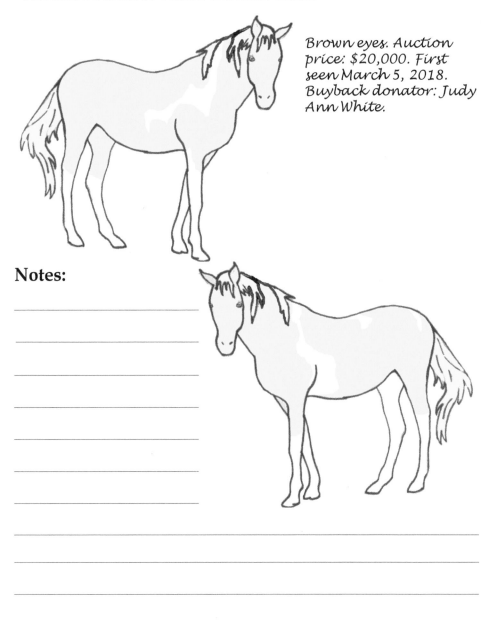

Brown eyes. Auction price: $20,000. First seen March 5, 2018. Buyback donator: Judy Ann White.

Notes:

Judy's Sunshine

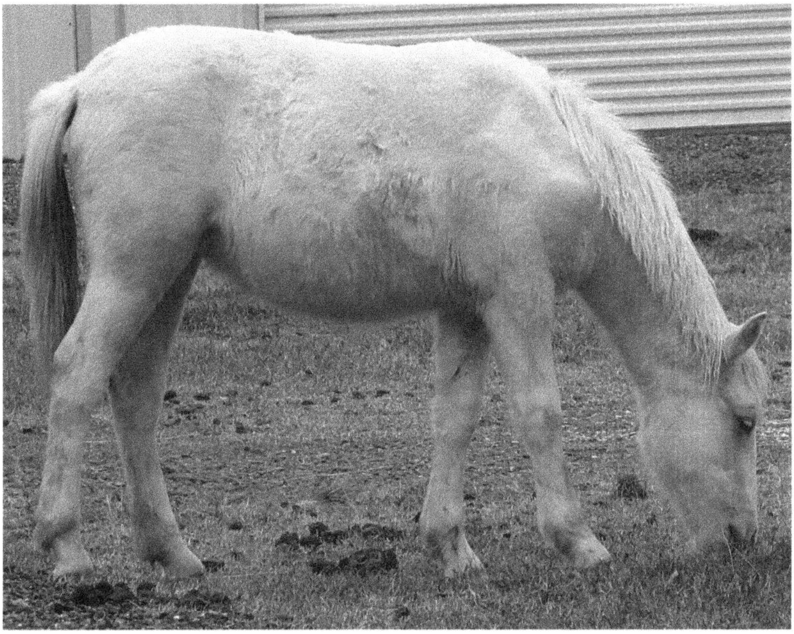

Tornado's Prince of Tides

Prince
stallion birth year: 2007 brand: 07
TORNADO X SAND CHERRY

Brown eyes. Auction price: $17,500. Born April 7, 2007. Buyback donator: Buyback Babes.

Notes:

Tornado's Prince of Tides

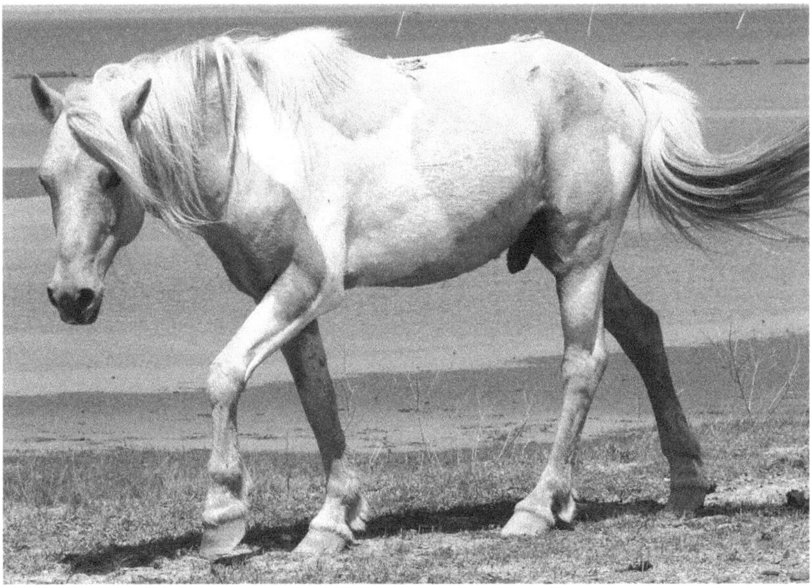

Mz Peg

Peggy
mare   birth year: 2020   brand: 20
TORNADO'S LEGACY x WHITE SADDLE

Brown eyes. Auction price: $25,000. First seen May 12, 2020. Buyback donor: George Panos in memory of Peggy McWhirt.

Notes:

Mz Peg

Little Miss Sunshine

Sunshine
mare birth year: 2015 brand: 15
TORNADO'S PRINCE OF TIDES X BAYBE

Brown eyes. Auction price: $5,300. Born July 3, 2015. Buyback donator: Joanne Niland and Nancie Oleynik.

Notes:

Little Miss Sunshine

Whisper of Living Legend

Whisper
mare birth year: 2000 brand: 00
NORTH STAR x LIVING LEGEND

Brown eyes. Born July 4, 2000. Buyback donator: David and Elizabeth Moore. Alternate sire: Rainbow Warrior.

Notes:

Whisper of Living Legend

Jigsaw's Little Miss Skeeter

Skeeter
mare birth year: 2018 brand: 18
TORNADO'S LEGACY x CODY'S LITTLE JIGSAW PUZZLE

Brown eyes. Auction price: $11,500. First seen May 4, 2018.

Notes:

Jigsaw's Little Miss Skeeter

Palomino Pinto

Sundance

mare birth year: 2012 brand: none
WH NIGHTWIND x WALNUT HILL'S SAND STORM

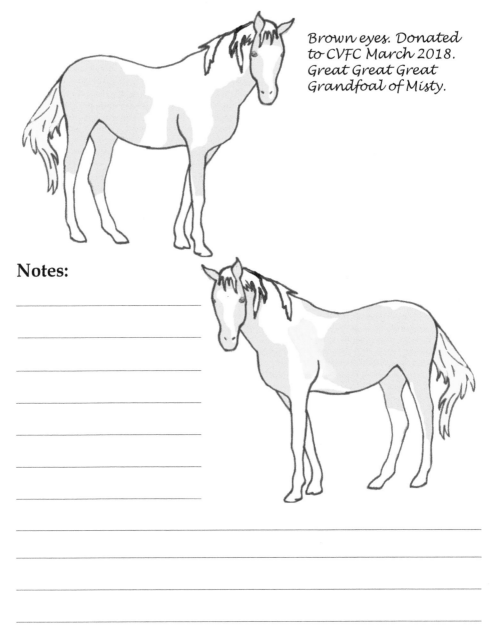

Brown eyes. Donated to CVFC March 2018. Great Great Great Grandfoal of Misty.

Notes:

Sundance

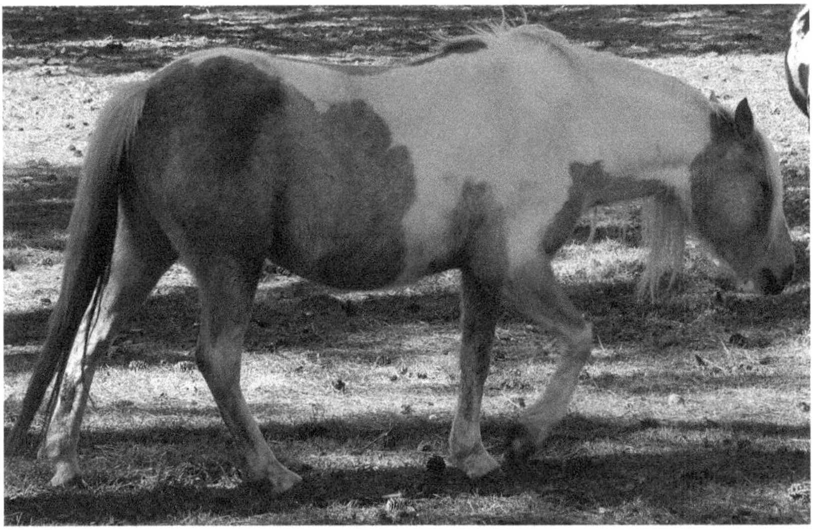

Palomino Pinto

Marina's Marsh Mallow

Marsh Mallow
mare   birth year: 2014   brand: 14
TORNADO'S PRINCE OF TIDES x FIFTEEN FRIENDS OF FRECKLES

Brown eyes. Auction price: $7,000. Buyback donator: Cassou family.

Notes:

Marina's Marsh Mallow

Palomino Pinto

Lorna Dune

mare birth year: 2013 brand: 13

DON LEONARD STUD X JESSICA'S SEA STAR SANDY

Brown eyes. Auction price: $6,200. Born May 5, 2013. Buyback donator: Kathleen Cahall.

Notes:

Lorna Dune

Close Family Index

Alphabetical Index

Alphabetical Index

Alphabetical Index

Alphabetical Index

Stallion Index

Brand Index

CPSIA information can be obtained
at www.ICGtesting.com
Printed in the USA
JSHW032039260321
12968JS00003B/15

9 780984 239221